1779 SEL

D1577354

WITHDRAWN
FROM STOCK
QMUL LIBRARY

0160090
3.10.88

Corneille, Tasso
and Modern Poetics

CORNEILLE, TASSO AND MODERN POETICS

A. Donald Sellstrom

Ohio State University Press
Columbus

Copyright © 1986 by the Ohio State University Press
All Rights Reserved.

Library of Congress Cataloging in Publication Data

Sellstrom, A. Donald
  Corneille, Tasso, and modern poetics.
  Bibliography:
  Includes index.
  1. Corneille, Pierre, 1606-1684—Criticism and interpretation.
2. Corneille, Pierre, 1606-1684—Knowledge—Literature.   3. Tasso,
Torquato, 1544-1595—Influence—Corneille.   4. Poetics.   5. Epic
poetry—History and criticism.   6. Classical poetry—History and
criticism.   I. Title.
PQ1779.S46   1986   842'.4   86-2539
  ISBN 0-8142-0410-4

For Eleanor

TABLE OF CONTENTS

Acknowledgments

THE IDEA THAT A SIGNIFICANT LINK MIGHT EXIST BETWEEN Torquato Tasso and Pierre Corneille came to me unexpectedly in the fall of 1978 as I was reading Mario Praz's book *On Neoclassicism*. A sentence-long quotation from the *Discorsi del poema eroico* jumped out at me: "Broken lines, entering one into the other . . . make the language magnificent and sublime." That this fine point in the theory of heroic style was not original with Tasso made no difference; I connected it immediately in my own mind with a number of audacious run-on lines in Corneille's fourth Roman play, *La Mort de Pompée*, lines that had long struck me as anomalous both in the playwright's own practice and in that of the French classicists in general. Thanks to being on leave at the time, I was free to follow up on the hunch and, accordingly, set about making a cursory first acquaintance with the great Italian poet and critic. In the end, the question of run-on lines would drop out of the picture entirely; in the process of reading the *Discorsi*, however, I proved to have stumbled on a text that would shed new light not only on *La Mort de Pompée* but, eventually and in conjunction with other texts of a theoretical or poetical nature, on several other of the playwright's best known works as well. The intuition, if that is what it was, that I experienced in happening on the sentence from Tasso was not quite like the "click" that Leo Spitzer spoke of in his famous essay on linguistics and literary history. It enabled me, nevertheless, to break into the hermeneutic circle—with what results it is now up to others to say.

Since 1978, I have incurred other debts both to individuals and to institutions. Among Corneille scholars, those whose works lay closest to my own line of inquiry were Marc Fumaroli and Marie-Odile Sweetser, both of whom at various times and in different ways lent encouragement. To Professor Sweetser I am grateful in particular for suggestions helping me, at an important juncture, to broaden the original focus of my study.

The University Research Institute of the University of Texas supported my work with a typing grant and, later, a publication grant, for both of which I hereby express my appreciation. The continued support of colleagues, friends, and family in Austin has been of crucial importance throughout. I should like especially to thank: Michel Dassonville, for having offered good advice on organizational matters; Elisabeth Herrington and Karen Kelton, for typing the several versions of my work as it progressed toward its final form; and, not least, my wife, Eleanor, and our children, without whose moral support through the years it would have been difficult, if not impossible, to persevere.

Parts of my argument concerning Tasso's influence on Corneille have appeared elsewhere, most recently in two papers read in France and later published: one in connection with a symposium held in the Spring of 1983 on "Le Mécénat en France avant Colbert" ("La *Théodore* de Corneille ou le statut social de l'écrivain"); the other in the context of the celebration in the fall of 1984 of the tercentenary of Corneille's death ("Corneille, émule du Tasse"). The subject matter of these papers has been entirely recast here, however. Chapter 5, on the other hand, incorporates virtually unchanged most of the text of an article published in 1982 in *PMLA* ("*La Mort de Pompée*: Roman History and Tasso's Theory of Christian Epic"). I am indebted to the editors of *PMLA* for permission to republish that material here.

Introduction

THE 1653 INVENTORY OF ART OBJECTS AND FINE FURNITURE belonging to Cardinal Mazarin contains the description of some twenty-two cabinets. One of these is said to have been decorated with "dix tableaux de mignature" depicting Apollo and the nine Muses and with "les portraicts de deux poètes anciens, et deux modernes" (d'Aumale, p. 252). In all probability this is the same cabinet as the one to which Charles Perrault referred at the end of the century in a biographical article on Corneille (in *Les Hommes illustres qui ont paru en France pendant ce siècle*):

> Tout Paris a vu un cabinet de pierres de rapport fait à Florence, et dont on avait fait présent au cardinal Mazarin, où, entre les divers ornements dont il est enrichi, on avait mis aux quatre coins les médailles ou les portraits des quatre plus grands poètes qui aient jamais paru dans le monde, savoir Homère, Virgile, Le Tasse et Corneille. (Mongrédien, p. 356)

The iconographical message of this cabinet is not hard to read up to a point. The cabinet very clearly not only celebrates the accomplishments of Corneille, it proposes a view of the history of poetry itself. This history is one of the transfer of poetic hegemony, as represented in each case by a single preeminent poet, from Greece, to Rome, to Italy, and finally to France. Corneille and French literature in general are seen as both inheriting a rich legacy from the past and reaffirming the highest sanctions of poetry for the present. The history of poetry is seen also to entail transference from the ancient world to the modern era, each world being represented by a pair of poets. This arrangement acknowledges the success of Renaissance efforts to reestablish a literary tradition rooted in antiquity. Because of its perfect symmetry, the decoration on the cabinet may also imply closure and retrospection, as if a divine equation had been completed and history had arrived at its full term.

If this much is clear, the rest is not. And what is most problematical of all is Corneille's relationship to the other three poets. Vergil won renown in large part by emulating Homer, and

Tasso in turn by emulating Vergil. Does the cabinet imply that Corneille has extended the line by emulation of Tasso? And Tasso's modernity rested above all on the fact that he had Christianized the Vergilian epic. Are we to assume by extrapolation that Corneille is a "modern" in the same sense as Tasso, that his plays somehow embody a decorum or ethic opposed to an earlier decorum or ethic? Finally, there is the question why Corneille, a playwright, is compared to three epic poets. Is this anomaly accidental and therefore of little interest, or does it perhaps point to something that for the time being escapes understanding?

The core of the argument I develop in this study is that Corneille did in fact set out to emulate Tasso (and secondarily Vergil also), although he never acknowledges the fact and indeed never even mentions the Italian poet's name. I intend to show, moreover, that he emulated Tasso in such a way as to enable us to read a number of his most important works (not restricted just to *Polyeucte* and *Théodore*) as "modern" in the Tassoan sense and, moreover, that he had a very conscious purpose in crossing a generic frontier in order to join forces with the epic tradition in poetry.

This thesis is new, but it draws on previous scholarship in three well-established fields. Two of these are Franco-Italian literary and cultural relations in the decades leading up to the Quarrel of the *Cid* and the Christian or providential dimensions of Corneille's theater. The scholars to whom I am indebted in these areas include Marc Fumaroli, Bernard Weinberg, Chandler B. Beall, and Joyce G. Simpson, on the one hand; Marie-Odile Sweetser, Jacques Maurens, André Stegmann, and Germain Poirier on the other. What I add to their work lies in the nature of specifying Italian influence as it exerts itself on Corneille and linking the playwright's "modernism" with a particular Italian source, Tasso.

Corneille's emulation of Tasso begins in the Quarrel of the *Cid* and is reflected above all in the tragedies he wrote from *Horace* to *Héraclius*. I pay special attention to four of these plays—*Polyeucte, La Mort de Pompée, Théodore,* and *Héraclius*—because they mark the most important stages of the development of that emulation; but I try to integrate the intervening plays into the argument as well. And I conclude with a chapter designed to confirm the thesis of emulation by examining it somewhat obliquely from two complementary angles: from the point of view of images incorporated into certain of the plays from the Quarrel of the *Cid*, and from the point of view of the "Discours de la tragédie" of 1660.

The third area of scholarship on which I rely consists of studies that stress the interrelationship of the plays themselves and the dialectics of Corneille's whole career as a playwright. Here, I think particularly of Marie-Odile Sweetser's *La Dramaturgie de Corneille* and Serge Doubvrovsky's *Corneille et la dialectique du héros*, very different works, but both quite sensitive to how much inspiration Corneille draws from himself and how often he builds one play on the accumulated logic of earlier plays. My study is restricted to the production of a short but crucial period—the decade, 1637–47, during which the playwright earned his reputation as "le grand Corneille." Within this period I follow a dialectical development that is concerned both with emulation and with "modernism" and that, once understood, sheds light on the question of why Corneille, a playwright, is compared to three epic poets in the decorative motif of the Mazarin cabinet.

The Quarrel of the *Cid*, a major vehicle for the entry into France of Italian ideas on poetry (Searles, p. 388), is the initial stimulus for Corneille's emulation of Tasso. It is, therefore, with the Quarrel that I begin.

Corneille, Tasso
and Modern Poetics

CHAPTER I
Motives for Emulation: The Quarrel of the *Cid*

IN THE DEDICATORY LETTER FOR *LA SUIVANTE*, CORNEILLE writes: "Je ne me suis jamais imaginé avoir mis rien au jour de parfait, je n'espère pas même y pouvoir jamais arriver; je fais néanmoins mon possible pour en approcher, et les plus beaux succès des autres ne produisent en moi qu'une vertueuse émulation, qui me fait redoubler mes efforts afin d'en avoir de pareils" (*Oeuvres,* 2:118). This statement is of interest for several reasons. For one thing, it seems to mark a change in Corneille's attitude toward his colleagues and perhaps also toward his art. Written at the height of the Quarrel over the *Cid*,[1] it is too tentative to constitute a real manifesto, but it clearly looks forward to something beyond the immediate context. The playwright had precipitated the Quarrel by the publication of the "Excuse à Ariste," in which he had adopted a rather arrogantly independent posture. Now, a few months later, he reverses himself and, in a gesture of conciliatory good will toward rivals like Mairet and Scudéry, presents himself as belonging to a brotherhood of poets. The business of this society of playwrights, as Corneille sees it, is moreover very serious. It involves no less than the arduous pursuit of perfection, with each individual poet vying to do his share toward the realization of a single great and noble dream.

More than twenty years later, as he girded himself to resume a career long interrupted, the playwright was to speak again of emulation and the search for perfection. The occasion was the poem he addressed to Foucquet, who had urged him to come out of retirement:

> Choisis-moi seulement quelque nom dans l'histoire
> Pour qui tu veuilles place au temple de la Gloire,
> Quelque nom favori qu'il te plaise arracher
> A la nuit de la tombe, aux cendres du bûcher.
> Soit qu'il faille ternir ceux d'Enée et d'Achille
> Par un noble attentat sur Homère et Virgile,
> Soit qu'il faille obscurcir par un dernier effort
> Ceux que j'ai sur la scène affranchis de la mort:
> Tu me verras le même, et je te ferai dire,
> Si jamais pleinement ta grande âme m'inspire,
> Que dix lustres et plus n'ont pas tout emporté
> Cet assemblage heureux de force et de clarté,
> Ces prestiges secrets de l'aimable imposture
> Qu'à l'envi m'ont prêtée et l'art et la nature.
> (*Oeuvres,* 6:122–23, ll. 37–50)

As in the dedicatory letter for *La Suivante,* so here Corneille pictures himself engaged in a struggle to exceed in the future what others, including his own younger self, have done in the past. There is the same sense of high purpose as before, the same emphasis on competition, the same eagerness to undertake challenge. The playwright has become more sure of himself, however; and the rivals he invokes in Homer and Vergil are the most illustrious conceivable. This later text serves to confirm and to expand the implications of the earlier text. It suggests that the call to emulation announced at the time that *La Suivante* appeared stayed with Corneille for a long time, but that the parameters of emulation changed, as the playwright looked beyond the Paris of his closest rivals to the universal history of poetry and of poets.

The crux of the argument that I intend to develop in what follows is that Corneille came to emulate above all Torquato Tasso, and that the plays that earned the French playwright his reputation as "le grand Corneille" were part of a long, sustained effort to duplicate, not the particular modes, but the overall sense of the Italian epic poet's earlier achievement. Such a thesis is no doubt surprising, in view of the fact that Corneille nowhere mentions Tasso or any of his works. I am convinced, nevertheless, that it was the example of Tasso that inspired Corneille to look beyond the rivalry with Mairet and Scudéry to consider poetry as something belonging to the world in general and to history. This hypothesis will have to be tested in the plays themselves, beginning with *Horace*. First, however, we need to know in what context and for what particular reasons Corneille could have been attracted to Tasso; and for that we must turn to the Quarrel of the *Cid.*

Tasso's fame, secure in France during his lifetime, stood even higher perhaps in the decade 1630–40, with which we are here concerned. Universally hailed as the greatest poet of the modern era, he was much admired also as a critic-theorist. His works were readily available, both in the Italian original and in French translations. The years preceding the Quarrel had seen the publication of French versions not only of the *Gerusalemme liberata* but also of the poet's two plays, *Aminta* and *Torrismondo*, as well as some of the *Dialoghi* and part of the *Discorsi.*[2] *Torrismon* had been one of the great successes of the 1635 season at the Marais. Corneille's theater. The translator, Vion d'Alibray, was a fellow Norman and perhaps a friend. The preface he wrote, when it came time to publish *Torrismon*, attests as well as anything else to the exceptionally high regard in which Tasso was then held. For d'Alibray not only praises Tasso himself, he quotes the praises of others: beginning with Paolo Beni, "[qui] a monstré l'advantage que sa Hierusalem avoit sur l'Aenéide," going on to Du Bartas, for whom Tasso was "le premier en honneur, & le dernier en aage," and coming finally to Balzac, who is quoted as saying that "Virgile est cause que le Tasse n'est pas le premier, & le Tasse, que Virgile n'est pas le seul."[3] A young poet bent on achieving the highest excellence in his art could not afford to overlook Tasso. Tasso was the standard by which others who came after were going to be judged.

One finds this idea of Tasso as master poet reflected in the fascinating correspondence of Philippe Fortin de la Hoguette concerning the *Cid.* Stationed at the fortress of Blaye at the time the play opened in Paris, La Hoguette had procured one of the first copies of the work through his Paris friend, Jacques Dupuy. He and his fellow officers were so enthralled by the *Cid* that they did more that read it: they acted it out. His enthusiasm survives receipt of the startling news a few weeks later that in Paris critics have begun to attack the play:

Pour moi je confesse de n'avoir jamais vu une plus vive image des vrais sentiments de l'honneur et de l'amour, qui sont les deux mobiles de toutes les plus grandes actions des hommes. Ce n'en est pas l'image seulement, c'en est l'âme. Si je ne m'abuse, je suis impénitent, et trouve mieux mon compte d'errer avec le peuple et le badaud que d'être des raffineurs. Tout y est généreux jusques aux confidents, et merveilleux pour l'intelligence du théâtre.   (Mongrédien, p. 64)[4]

La Hoguette defends the *Cid* by comparing it, favorably, with the most canonical poems he can think of. The *Cid*, he says, most certainly has flaws ("de le voir égal partout, c'est lui désirer trop d'embonpoint"), but the world's greatest poems would appear flawed, too, if they were to be viewed in the same harsh light: "De dire qu'il y a des défauts en l'élocution, si nous avions la pureté des langues grecque, latine et italienne comme de la nôtre, et que nous voulussions égratigner sur Homère, Virgile et le Tasse, je doute qu'on en fît un jugement plus favorable. . . ." La Hoguette does not mean to consecrate the young playwright prematurely; but he has discerned in him rare poetic qualities, and he is not afraid to hail him as a future candidate for the most exalted of ranks in the pantheon: "Ce n'est pas offenser les Anciens que de leur donner un concurrent. Honneur leur soit rendu, et aux Modernes aussi qui seront un jour Anciens, s'ils le méritent." The fact that the *Gerusalemme liberata* (like the *Aeneid* and the *Iliad*) is an epic poem whereas the *Cid* is a play poses no problem for La Hoguette. It is enough for him, it would seem, that both are cast in the heroic mold. If asked, he could no doubt have added that Aristotle had treated dramatic and epic poetry together in the *Poetics*, as indeed Tasso himself had also done in the *Discorsi*; but he is obviously less interested in explaining than he is in affirming. And what he affirms, essentially, is that Corneille could become in a sense the French Tasso, just as Tasso had become the Italian Vergil, and Vergil, the Roman Homer.

Later on in the Quarrel, a somewhat different kind of emulation comes into view; and Tasso and Corneille are compared, not as heroic poets, but rather as participants in important literary controversies. The *doctes*, who were attacking the *Cid* on Aristotelian grounds, had learned their Aristotle as much from Cinquecento commentaries as from the *Poetics* itself. Indeed, an

American scholar from the beginning of this century was able to propose Italian "sources" for most of the major points made for or against Corneille in the pages of the *Sentiments de l'Académie française*.[5] It was common knowledge, too, among French poetic theorists that the Cinquecento had been punctuated by four great literary quarrels and that through these quarrels ancient theory and modern practice had confronted one another in a continuing dialectic that produced important changes in both. The first of these great quarrels had concerned Dante and the *Commedia*; the next, *Canace* and dramatic poetry. The two most recent controversies, which for that reason were uppermost in French minds, had centered on the *Gerusalemme* of Tasso and its relation to Ariostos' *Orlando furioso* and on the *Pastor fido* of Guarini. Chapelain's library, we know, was well stocked with books and treatises not only on the *Poetics* but on every one of these Italian quarrels of the century before (Searles, pp. 364–65).[6]

Chapelain and Scudéry both see Italian debates as part of the background of the debate raging in France, but they interpret the current situation and its implications for the future quite differently. Scudéry invokes the memory of both Tasso and Guarini in the course of his first letter to the Academy and of Tasso alone in a follow-up letter. He holds the *Cid* to be a false masterpiece, in contrast to the true masterpieces of the *Gerusalemme* and the *Pastor fido*. And he declares Corneille to be the exact opposite of Tasso in his reaction to critical attack. These two letters taken together show that, in Scudéry's mind, the Quarrel of the *Cid* could never be considered the equivalent of an Italian quarrel. It seemed to him instead a perfect travesty of the real thing and nothing more than that. Chapelain, writing later in the name of the Academy, is much more sanguine, however. He opens the *Sentiments* with an apology for criticism suggested by Guarini, or at least by the quarrel over the *Pastor fido* (Searles, p. 366). This apology argues for the usefulness of literary controversy as a means of discovering new truth about poetry. Chapelain no doubt is interested in countering the idea that the Quarrel over the *Cid* has been the persecution of the *Cid*. His faith in criticism and in progress toward perfect understanding of poetry seems genuine, however. In any event, he transforms the literary quarrel into something quite heroic, the equivalent in fact of the kind of formal *duellum* found in *Horace*. No matter how violent the encounter, it will serve the cause of truth, in Chapelain's opinion, provided only that all participants maintain the proper decorum and enter the fray not for personal advantage or out of animosity toward others, but solely in hope of aiding the triumph of truth. Conducted according to such rules, the literary quarrel becomes "une espece de guerre qui est avantageuse pour tous, lorsqu'elle se fait civilement et que les armes empoisonnées y sont defenduës," or "une course, où celuy qui emporte le prix semble ne l'avoir poursuivy que pour en faire un present à son rival." The rivalry among participants may be intense, but it is never personal. It produces only "des contestations honnestes" and "[une] heureuse violence [par laquelle] on a tiré la Verité du fond des abysmes" (Gasté, pp. 356–57).

Quarrels of this ideal nature have been fought, says Chapelain, throughout history. He calls attention particularly to the beneficial results of the last two Italian quarrels:

> . . . Parmy les Modernes il s'en est esmeu de tres-favorables pour les Lettres, et. . . la Poësie seroit aujourd'huy bien moins parfaite qu'elle n'est, sans les contestations qui se sont formées sur les ouvrages des plus celebres Autheurs des derniers Temps. En effect nous en avons la principale obligation aux agreables differens qu'ont produit la Hierusalem et le Pastor Fido, c'est à dire les Chef-d'oeuvres des deux plus grands Poëtes de de-là les Monts; apres lesquels peu de gens auroient bonne grace de murmurer contre la Censure, et de s'offencer d'avoir une aventure pareille à la leur. (Gasté, p. 357)

These last remarks are clearly aimed at Corneille, who had protested the intervention of the Academy. It is significant, however, that Chapelain, far from sharing Scudéry's estimation of the Quarrel as only a poor travesty of the real thing, now holds out hope that the controversy over the *Cid* in time will prove just as beneficial to the advancement of poetry as the heroic encounters in Italy at the end of the Cinquecento. Imbued himself with a high sense of emulation, Chapelain would like nothing better than to think that he had helped raise the Quarrel of the *Cid* to the level of the quarrels over the *Gerusalemme* and the *Pastor fido*. He and the Academy had done their part, he thought; it remained to be seen whether Corneille would follow suit. From a different point of view and for different reasons, then, Chapelain arrived at the same conclusion as La Hoguette: Corneille was a good candidate for greatness, a worthy "concurrent" for the highest of poetic prizes.

Corneille was perceived, then, to have at least two things in common with Tasso, the acknowledged prince of modern poets: a rare gift for heroic poetry and the honor of having been at the center of a momentous literary dispute. The closing pages of the *Sentiments* map out a plan of artistic action that, I think, serves to bring Corneille into relationship with Tasso in yet a third way. These pages deal almost exclusively with heroic decorum and the choice of a proper subject for poetry. One must ask why it is that Chapelain ignores completely the question of verisimilitude, which had preoccupied him often in the past and which had figured prominently throughout the Quarrel and, therefore, in the main body of the *Sentiments*. The answer, I think, lies in the remarks he makes about audience reaction to the *Cid*: they were so enthralled by the story, he says, that they lost all power to discriminate the good in the play from the bad.[7] Ironically, this suspension of critical faculties was exactly what Chapelain himself had said, in the famous "Lettre sur les vingt-quatre heures," was the aim of illusionist art and, specifically, of techniques of verisimilitude in the theater. The idea was, he said, to induce such a powerful illusion of reality on stage that the spectators would cease to think of the action as unreal and so be receptive to experiencing the full emotional effect of the play. It is quite likely, I think, that if not the Quarrel, at least the *Cid* itself opened Chapelain's eyes to a new truth about verisimilitude: namely, that it was a kind of poetic rhetoric and, like rhetoric, was dangerous when not coupled securely to high ethical aims. If the critic puts the whole of his emphasis on decorum at the end of the *Sentiments*, it can only mean, in any event, that in Chapelain's opinion Corneille has learned the lesson of theatrical illusion well enough already but needs advice, perhaps urgently, on the matter of *bienséances*.

Chapelain is intent, above all, on stressing the poet's personal responsibility in the selection and treatment of a subject. The authority of history and the authority of earlier poets who may have treated the same subject not only do not bind a poet, the poet is obligated, instead, to honor the highest authority (aesthetic or moral, but particularly moral) that happens to exist *at the moment he writes.* For just as Chapelain had seen the great literary quarrels as contributing to the progressive discovery of truth about poetry, so here he conceives of an evolution in ethical (and, occasionally, also aesthetic) perception, a succession of authorities or jurisidictions or dispensations that, over time, bring mankind, ideally, ever closer to perfection. In this constantly shifting aesthetico-ethical landscape, what once appeared right, what once was authorized, may in time be seen as faulty and lacking in essential sanction. Though the poet necessarily draws from the past, he has the responsibility, *qua* poet, to adjust the past, if necessary, to the present:

> . . . Les fautes mesmes des Anciens qui semblent devoir estre respectées pour leur vieillesse, ou si on l'ose dire, pour leur immortalité, ne peuvent pas defendre les [mêmes fautes reprises par des Modernes]. Il est vray que celles la ne sont presque considerées qu'avec reverence, d'autant que les unes estant faittes devant les regles, sont nées libres et hors de leur jurisdiction, et que les autres par une longue durée ont comme acquis une prescription legitime. Mais cette faveur qui à peine met à couvert ces grands Hommes, ne passe point jusques à leurs successeurs. Ceux qui viennent apres eux heritent bien de leurs richesses, mais non pas de leurs privileges, et les vices d'Euripide ou de Seneque ne sçauroient faire approuver ceux de Guillen de Castro. (Gasté, p. 415)

The basic fault in the *Cid*, according to Chapelain, lay in the denouement: that is, in the marriage of Rodrigue and Chimène. It makes no difference to him that history, first, and Guillén de Castro, second, had recorded that event before Corneille put it into his own play. He holds Corneille responsible for everything in the *Cid*, whatever its source may be. The historian, he says, is bound to respect factual truth; the poet must often violate it, because his first allegiance is never to truth, but always to "la bienséance": "Mais comme cette Verité [de l'historien] à peu de credit dans l'Art des beaux mensonges, nous pensons qu'à son tour elle [la Vérité] y doit ceder à la bien-seance, qu'estre inventeur et imitateur n'est icy qu'une mesme chose, et que le Poëte François qui nous a donné le Cid, est coupable de toutes les fautes qu'il n'y a pas corrigées" (Gasté, p. 416).

The conception of poetry that emerges from the opening

and closing sections of the *Sentiments* is all of one piece: in the march toward perfection, the critic and the poet join forces to overcome error. Literary quarrels are beneficial because they root out error and reveal more truth; the poet, for his part, must invent even as he imitates and correct whatever faults he is able to discern in the material he has chosen to use. The corollary to the idea that the poet owes primary allegiance to decorum is, therefore, that he must either choose a highly decorous subject to begin with or else be prepared to correct or rectify the subject in order to bring it into conformity with the current highest perception of decorum.

The parameters of this program of literary rectification can be understood more fully if we look at what Chapelain has to say about the denouement in the main body of the *Sentiments*. For one thing, he gives several examples of how the faulty denouement could have been corrected. More important for our purposes here, he is at pains to justify the poet's right to introduce changes, because Scudéry in the *Observations* had specifically denied the poet any licence to tamper with historical fact (Gasté, pp. 76–77; 368). Chapelain's argument does not differ from what he says in the conclusion: a poet is not a historian, but if he changes his material, he must change it for the better, morally speaking. What is interesting is the authorities he cites in connection with this argument and the way he uses them. The authorities are Vergil above all, but also Tasso. Both poets are cited as having introduced significant changes in chronology: Vergil, in order to make Aeneas and Dido contemporaries; Tasso, in order to allow Godefroy de Bouillon and Rinaldo to fight in the same Crusade (Gasté, pp. 368–71). Vergil, he says, also made another kind of change: he took the historical Dido, who was chaste, and made her into "une femme impudique." Some critics, Chapelain adds, have criticized Vergil for his treatment of Dido; he himself does not. He refrains from passing judgment partly out of respect for Vergil, but mainly because his argument does not require that he do so. The point he wants to make in juxtaposing Dido and Chimène is that in the case of the *Cid* Corneille easily could have altered the historical facts for the better, and no one would have dreamed of holding it against him:

[Les critiques de Virgile] ne l'ont pas accusé proprement d'avoir peché contre l'Art en changeant la verité, mais contre les bonnes moeurs en diffamant une personne, qui avoit mieux aymé mourir que de vivre diffamée. Il en fust arrivé tout au contraire dans le changement qu'on eust peu faire au sujet du Cid puis qu'on eust corrigé les mauvaises moeurs qui se trouvent dans l'histoire, et qu'on les eust renduës bonnes par la Poësie pour l'utilité du Public.   (Gasté, p. 369)

Chapelain does not say so, but one may assume he would think also that, if Corneille or any other modern poet were to treat the story of Dido and Aeneas, he would have to rectify the story and make it conform to the body of truths available to the modern, Christian artist. Vergil, a pagan, was not bound by an authority that came into the world only after his death. Ignorance excuses, but it does not justify; and Corneille could not duplicate Vergil's "fault" with impunity. Seeing it as a fault, he would have to correct it.

If Chapelain cites two epic poets in this crucial section of the *Sentiments,* very probably it is because the theory of rectification, if one may call it that, had been worked out in relation to the epic, not in relation to tragedy. Most likely of all, he was drawing on his knowledge of the theory of the Christian epic as Tasso himself had outlined it in books 2 and 3 of the *Discorsi del poema eroico.* Tasso's fame rested on the fact that he had Christianized the ancient epic, thus, in effect, bringing it to its final perfection. The Italian poet's theory supported his practice. He saw the traditional forms and genres inherited from antiquity as retaining their original validity because they corresponded to unchanging aspects of the human psyche. The ethical and religious systems of the Ancients, on the other hand, had lost their authority altogether with the divine revelation of the Christian truths. His advice to would-be epic poets, accordingly, was to adhere to the traditional form of the epic but to infuse it with the new true Christian spirit. The epic hero henceforth had to be Christian, he thought; and he was to be motivated above all by love instead of by wrath. The terms *fault, error, correction,* and *rectification* that loom so important in Chapelain's thought are new and reflect a heightened sense of ideological and psychological strain characteristic of the Counter Reformation in France. Except for the fact that Tasso had spoken only about the epic, the message remained basically the same, however: the modern poet could accept the authority of the Ancients in matters of aesthetics, but he could not follow their example in regard to ethics or religion. Chapelain does not refer to Tasso in the last pages of the *Sentiments* as he did in the introduction. There can be little doubt that he is thinking of him, however, and that he is proposing the Italian poet to Corneille not only as an illustrious forebear in the history of literary quarrels but as a model to follow in perfecting heroic decorum in his theater.

Chapelain joins La Hoguette and Scudéry, then, in evoking the name and the prestige of Tasso in connection with Corneille. La Hoguette did so in order to praise the young French playwright; Scudéry, to damn him; Chapelain, to goad him to a higher level of poetic consciousness. All three held up the author of the *Gerusalemme* as an ideal object of emulation, Scudéry doing so, however, only to deny to Corneille the possibility of attainment. Corneille probably never saw La Hoguette's laudatory letters, and he could not act on Chapelain's advice until it came time to write *Horace*. He seems to have taken up Scudéry's challenge, however, even before the end of the Quarrel, and in such a way as to prefigure, as it were, something of the course he would take after the Quarrel.

Let us go back to the two letters that Scudéry wrote to the Academy. Scudéry had two reasons for grievance as regards Corneille. First, it seemed to him that the success of the *Cid* was unwarranted. He had tried to deal with that situation by writing and publishing the *Observations*, which he expected would lead Corneille into a theoretical debate on the play. Corneille had refused to debate, however; not only that, in a short "Lettre apologitique," he had dismissed the *Observations* as irrelevant ("Si un volume d'Observations ne suffit faites-en encore cinquante") and had declared in closing that public approbation was all the apology the play needed or would ever get. Scudéry dealt with this second blow by turning to the Academy and asking that it reply to the *Observations*, inasmuch as Corneille himself did not want to. Scudéry's resentment at the refusal of Corneille to debate him is expressed most forcefully in his second letter to the Academy, which he begins with a contrast between Tasso's *Apologia della Gerusalemme liberata*, a reply to the Accademia della Crusca, and Corneille's "Lettre apologitique du sieur Corneille, contenant sa responce aux Observations faites par le Sieur Scuderi sur le Cid." He starts with a quotation in Italian from the opening paragraph of the *Apologia*: "Io non mi dolgo, che hab biano cercato d'impedirmi questo honore, che m'era fatto d'al vulgo, perche di nissuna cosa regioneuole mi debbo dolere: piu tosto dourei lamentarmi di coloro, che inalzandomi doue non merito di salire, non hanno riguardo al precipitio" (Gasté, p. 219). This is followed immediately by a formal juxtaposing of the behavior of Tasso and that of Corneille in a like situation:

> Ce sont [là] les modestes paroles, par où le Tasse, le plus grand homme de son siecle, a commencé l'Apologie du plus beau de ses Ouvrages, contre la plus aigre, et la plus injuste Censure, qu'on fera peut-estre jamais: Monsieur Corneille, tesmoigne bien en ses Responses, qu'il est aussi loing de la moderation, que du merite de cet excellent Autheur, puis qu'au lieu de se donner l'humilité d'un Accusé, il occupe la place des Juges et se loge luy-mesme à ce premier lieu, où personne n'oseroit seulement dire qu'il pretend.

Corneille was to make only two more substantial public statements during the course of the Quarrel: the "Advertisse- ment au Besançonnois Mairet" and the dedicatory letter for *La Suivante*. In the "Advertissement" he adopted much the same truculent, condescending tone he had used in the earlier reply to Scudéry, but he did not sign his name to the document. The dedicatory letter, for its part, reflects an entirely new attitude on the part of the playwright. Before, he had treated Scudéry and Mairet as inferiors and had challenged them sarcastically to write as good a play as the *Cid* if they could. Now, as we saw at the beginning of the chapter, he speaks of wanting to engage these same rivals in a friendly competition from which he himself may hope to benefit: "Je ne me suis jamais imaginé avoir mis rien au jour de parfait, je n'espère pas même y pouvoir jamais arriver; je fais néanmoins mon possible pour en approcher, et les plus beaux succès des autres ne produisent en moi qu'une vertueuse émulation, qui me fait redoubler mes efforts afin d'en avoir de pareils" (*Oeuvres*, 2:118). Moreover, although he still affirms the idea that a playwright must first of all please his audience ("puisque nous faisons des poëmes pour être représentés, notre premier but doit être de plaire à la cour et au peuple"), he is now ready to recognize another requirement as also legitimate: "Il faut, s'il se peut, y ajouter les règles, afin de ne déplaire pas aux savants, et recevoir un applaudissement universel. . . . " These two statements mark a clear reversal in Corneille's public posture; and it may very well be that this reversal was prompted by Scudéry's remarks in his second letter to the Academy.[8]

Corneille's disclaimer concerning his ability to create anything perfect echoes the humility that Scudéry admired so much in the *Apologia* of Tasso. (Indeed, in the dedicatory letter of the *Apologia*, Tasso points out that, in the nature of things, poets will always fall short of perfection just as critics will often be quicker to blame than to praise.)[9] Nor in the circumstances is Corneille's desire to aim for universal approbation a sign of pride; on the contrary, it serves to recognize a point of view that the playwright had heretofore tended to ignore or to exclude. As a gesture of conciliatoriness and as a bid for consensus, the letter again reflects what Scudéry had held up as admirable in Tasso.[10]

The Quarrel of the *Cid* yields evidence, then, of a context in which it would make sense for Corneille to want to emulate Tasso, as well as evidence that he may actually have decided to do so in the dedication of *La Suivante*. It is interesting, moreover, to note that a degree of ambiguity and of secrecy already manifests itself at this early stage. Chapelain, we saw, cites Tasso at the beginning of the *Sentiments*, where he is talking about the glorious history of literary quarrels, but not at the end, when he is giving Corneille advice concerning the need to rethink the heroic decorum of his theater. The failure to mention the Italian poet at the end may be accidental and therefore of no great significance. It may point, however, to an unresolved tension in Chapelain's thought. Tasso, whom he admires greatly and whose place in the history of the epic looms very important for Chapelain, dealt with specifically Christian themes and advised the would-be modern epic poet to do the same. Chapelain argues for the enhancement of heroic decorum in the theater, but he never links that enhancement with Christianity. One may suspect that he refrains from mentioning Tasso at the end of the *Sentiments* because he senses that Tasso's authority for Christian subjects in heroic poetry cannot be extended from epic to tragedy, at least in France. The heightened decorum that he urges on Corneille is thus left somewhat ill defined and only implicitly Christian.

It is not hard to see reasons, on the other hand, why Corneille might have preferred not to mention Tasso in the dedication of *La Suivante*, even though, as I have suggested, he seems to be emulating him already. For one thing, to attribute his new-found moderation in debate to the example of Tasso would have been to credit Scudéry with that change also, inasmuch as Scudéry had brought up the exemplary nature of the *Apologia della Gerusalemme liberata* in the first place, in his second letter to the Academy. And though Corneille was striving to be conciliatory toward his opponents, there is no reason to think he would have wanted to go so far as to magnify the role of Scudéry in the Quarrel in the process. More generally, ordinary prudence could also have dictated discretion on the part of Corneille. Because of his remarks in the "Excuse à Ariste" his enemies already had accused him of inordinate pride. In the circumstances, if he had indicated an intention to emulate Tasso, who everyone agreed was the greatest of all modern poets, the playwright might well have exposed himself to ridicule and to charges of presumption that it would obviously be best to avoid.

Corneille and Chapelain both know that, like politics, art itself is often the art of the possible, or, to put it another way, that art can never be entirely divorced from the politics of art. In the matter that concerns us here, both men seem to recognize not only the desirability of some sort of emulation of Tasso but the need, for one reason or another, to be discreet about it at the same time. In any event, I hope to show in what follows that, from *Horace* to *Héraclius*, Corneille undertook in fact a secret emulation of Tasso, designed to accomplish for tragedy something of what the Italian poet was held to have achieved for the epic.

CHAPTER II

Polyeucte and Book Four
of the *Aeneid*

CORNEILLE'S RESPONSE TO THE CHALLENGE OF THE QUARrel can be read in the structure of his next three plays, which are probably also his greatest. The relationships of the individual plays to each other and to the concerns of the Quarrel are quite complex and will require considerable space to unravel. I intend to argue eventually that Corneille conceived of *Horace, Cinna,* and *Polyeucte* as a kind of trilogy or carefully interconnected group of plays that might qualify for consideration alongside the *Gerusalemme liberata* of Tasso as a major *oeuvre.* The trilogy does not come into existence, however, except with the last of the three plays, *Polyeucte,* which also shows the clearest, most direct relationship with the Quarrel. For this reason, I shall start with *Polyeucte* and, later on, relate it to *Horace* and *Cinna.* Concerning *Polyeucte* I shall argue, first, that Corneille wrote it as a Christian analogue of book 4 of the *Aeneid,* the episode of Aeneas and Dido; then, that it was the Quarrel of the *Cid* and Tasso together that led him to this rectification of Vergil.

Rectification may be defined as the process by which a playwright, through the introduction of substantial changes, can seek to enhance the decorum of a subject borrowed from history or literary tradition. In extreme cases it may allow him to salvage a subject that otherwise would be deemed too archaic, violent, or shocking for public taste. Formally, there would appear to be only two possible categories of rectification, depending on whether the playwright acknowledges or conceals the links between his own play and the source, or sources, that provide its subject matter.[1] *La Mort de Pompée* offers several examples of openly acknowledged rectification, the most striking of which concerns the character of Cléopâtre. Roman historians and Lucan, in the *Pharsalia*, all depict the Egyptian queen as a lascivious temptress; Corneille, as he explains in the Examen, paints her instead as nobly ambitious. He has, in other words, undertaken quite openly to rehabilitate the reputation of one of the most notorious women of the ancient world. The ostensible source of *Rodogune* is also history; and in the Avertissement to that play, Corneille cites a pertinent passage from Appian of Alexandria and then proceeds to indicate how and why he thought it wise to invoke the poet's right to modify historical fact. Appian's story narrates a long struggle for power—two sons against their mother, who kills one son and is forced by the other to drink poison. None of the principals is in any way noble. Corneille rehabilitates the character of both sons and, while preserving the queen's death by poisoning for a spectacular denouement, changes the incidents, or "acheminements," leading up to it. Most notably, he sees to it that the surviving son remains totally innocent of his mother's death; the queen still dies of poison, but it is self-administered. This rectification, like a number of others in the play, resembles the rectification of Cléopâtre in *Pompée*. There is, however, a major difference between *Rodogune* and *Pompée* in that the historical incidents in *Rodogune* are so obscure that no one would have noticed the playwright's changes if he had not called attention to them himself.

In the "Discours de la tragédie," Corneille at one point expresses dissatisfaction with Sophocles' treatment of the murder of Clytemnestra. He cannot tolerate ("je ne puis souffrir") that Orestes should kill Clytemnestra by design or that Electra should egg him on to such a horrible, unnatural act. These aspects of the story are totally inconsistent with the modern rule, unknown to the Ancients, that the main heroes should be sympathetic. Having detailed the deficiencies of *Electra*, Corneille proceeds then to explain how one might go about correcting them:

> Pour rectifier ce sujet à notre mode, il faudroit qu'Oreste n'eût dessein que contre Egisthe; qu'un reste de tendresse respectueuse pour sa mère lui en fît remettre la punition aux Dieux; que cette reine s'opiniâtrât à la protection de son adultère, et

qu'elle se mît entre son fils et lui si malheureusement qu'elle reçût le coup que ce prince voudroit porter à cet assassin de son père. Ainsi elle mourroit de la main de son fils, comme le veut Aristote, sans que la barbarie d'Oreste nout fît horreur, comme dans Sophocle, ni que son action méritât des Furies vengeresses pour le tourmenter, puisqu'il demeureroit innocent. (*Oeuvres,* 1:81)

It is obvious that the rectifications here go in exactly the same direction as the rectifications actually made in the historical sources of *Rodogune.* In fact, as Marc Fumaroli has shown in a brilliant article, *Rodogune* is like a palimpsest in which one can read at various levels and with varying degrees of clarity the traces of many literary and historical analogues ("Tragique païen et tragique chrétien," p. 629). To simplify somewhat, one can say that Corneille seems to have used the Hellenistic historical source—the story of the Syrian queen and her two sons—in order to conceal a more important connection between *Rodogune* and *Electra.* This is not the place to examine the possible motives for such a concealment. Suffice it to say that the playwright must have found it easier and safer to introduce radical changes into the story of an obscure Syrian queen than into the universally known story of Clytemnestra. Corneille would one day undertake to rectify *Oedipus Rex* quite openly, but only after he had long since become "le grand Corneille." To summarize, then, *La Mort de Pompée* illustrates openly acknowledged rectification, whereas *Rodogune* is an example of rectification in part concealed.

I have taken these examples of rectification from Corneille's later work, but the playwright did not wait until *Pompée* and *Rodogune* to practice rectification. A good example can be seen as early as *L'Illusion comique.* Corneille's previous work and first real tragedy had been *Médée,* in which the heroine's awful crime is preserved intact from antiquity, along with the ferocity of her hatred for Jason and for her rival, Créuse. A few months later, in *L'Illusion comique,* the playwright came back to the same subject matter; and, in the little tragedy of act 5—the tragedy in which Clindor and Isabelle act out the roles of Théagène and Hippolyte—he elaborated a hidden rectification of the Medea story.

The relevant action is contained in two scenes—5.3 and

4—the last of which Corneille dropped from the play after 1660. In the first scene, Hippolyte surprises her husband, Théagène, in a garden at night as he is awaiting the arrival of Rosine, a princess with whom he is determined to have an affair. The situation parallels the moment when Médée berates Jason for leaving her for Créuse. Indeed, at seven points in the exchange between husband and wife, it is clear that Corneille is actually borrowing arguments from Euripides.[2] Though Hippolyte echoes Médée from time to time and finds herself in a Medean situation, she is otherwise quite unlike her Greek counterpart, however. In particular she is far from vengeful. Indeed, toward the end of the confrontation, despairing of deflecting Théagène from his chosen path and fearing for him and for herself when the liaison is discovered, as surely it will be, she resolves very sadly to commit suicide.

If Hippolyte is thus a "rectified" version of Médée, Théagène becomes in turn a redeemed Jason. For not only is he so touched by his wife's love that he is converted suddenly to the cause of marital fidelity, he continues to defend this new cause when, a moment later, his mistress Rosine arrives. Scene 4 functions as a reprise of scene 3, but also as a corrective to it. Théagène is once more castigated as a faithless lover, but his situation has changed so that he appears excusable now: he is breaching a commitment to his mistress, but only in order to acknowledge a higher commitment to his wife. Just as we saw Corneille exonerate Antiochus for his mother's death in *Rodogune*, so here the playwright rehabilitates Jason by effectively expunging his guilt while retaining his crime. The paradigm allows for a major change in decorum without sacrifice of dramatic interest; and Corneille will make use of it in one form or another in his next four plays. Rodrigue, Horace, and Polyeucte, inasmuch as they prove "unfaithful" to a mistress, a friend, or a wife, can all be viewed as descendants of Jason—or rather of Théagène, for like Théagène, the redeemed Jason-figure of *L'Illusion*, they all have justifiable reasons for acting as they do. Cinna, who remains faithful to Emilie when he ought not to, is the exception that proves the rule; and the price he pays for not being bolder is to relinquish to Auguste his role as hero in the play: *Cinna, ou la Clémence d'Auguste.*

During the Quarrel of the *Cid*, the brunt of criticism fell not on Rodrigue's action in killing his mistress's father in a duel but rather on Chimène's failure to cease loving Rodrigue, and more specifically on her supposed acceptance of Rodrigue as husband at the end of the play.[3] The marriage of Rodrigue and Chimène, a historical fact, was obviously not in harmony with contemporary French ideas of decorum. Corneille knew he had a problem and attempted to deal with it by leaving the prospect of marriage somewhat in doubt. The maneuver seems to have satisfied the general public; but Scudéry, in his *Observations*, took the view that since it was historical, the marriage of the lovers could not be avoided. At the same time, it was so repugnant to morality that it rendered the whole subject intrinsically bad and totally unsuitable for the theater (Gasté, pp. 73–77). When Chapelain came to answer this criticism later on in the *Sentiments*, he granted that the subject was defective as treated by Corneille, but argued that the poet is always free to modify history and that Corneille's fault consequently lay not in choosing an unusable subject but in failing to change the subject so as to remove what was offensive in it: "Que si [le Poëte] est obligé de traitter une matiere historique de cette nature [non conforme à la raison], c'est alors qu'il la doit reduire aux termes de la bien-séance, sans avoir egard à la verité, et qu'il la doit plustost changer toute entiere que de luy laisser rien qui soit incompatible avec les regles de son Art; lequel se proposant l'idée universelle des choses, les espure des defaux et des irregularités particulières que l'histoire par la severité de ses loix est contrainte d'y souffrir." Chapelain goes on to suggest three ways in which Corneille might have altered the historical facts in order to recuperate the defective subject:

> De sorte qu'il y auroit eu sans comparaison moins d'inconvenient dans la disposition du Cid, de feindre contre la verité, ou que le Comte ne se fust pas trouvé à la fin le veritable Pere de Chimene, ou que contre l'opinion de tout le monde il ne fust pas mort de sa blessure, ou que le salut du Roy et du Royaume eust absolument dependu de ce mariage, pour compenser la violence que souffroit la Nature en cette occasion, par le bien que le Prince et son Estat en recevroit; tout cela, disonsnous, auroit esté plus pardonnable, que de porter sur la scene l'evenement tout pur et tout scandaleux, comme l'histoire le fournissoit.   (Gasté, p. 366)

These proposals, stated with little nuance, may sound slightly ridiculous; but basically they are not different from the kinds of changes that Corneille himself undertook in *L'Illusion* or that he would later introduce into *Pompée* and *Rodogune*. Unlike the disguised rectification of *Médée* in *L'Illusion*, however, the rectification that Chapelain has in mind here is one that would be openly acknowledged: Chimène would still be called Chimène. Corneille would not have been at fault if he had followed a course like this—or if he had taken the perhaps more expedient path of rejecting the subject outright. The two points that Chapelain wished to make were these: that Corneille did have a choice in the matter (which is what Scudéry had denied) and that, in any event, what the poet ought not to have done was to use the lovers' marriage unaltered—or, in the words of the *Sentiments*, to "l'exposer à la veuë du Peuple, sans l'avoir auparavant rectifié."

Now that we know what is meant by rectification, let us proceed to see whether it can be demonstrated that *Polyeucte* is a disguised rectification of the Aeneas-Dido story in book 4 of the *Aeneid*. In order to discern rectification, we must read the two texts together, as it were, and note a basic similarity against which certain divergences will stand out as particularly meaningful. The rectification will consist in the sum of those divergencies that tend toward an enhancement of decorum.

Both stories, the Christian play and the pagan epic, recount the exploits of a hero with a mission. Both heroes are in danger of neglecting this mission for love of a woman, and both are sent warnings not to dally. Both men heed these warnings, undertake the preparations necessary to accomplish their mission, and meanwhile try to hide their plans from the woman. The woman, when she finds out what is happening, confronts the hero with his "infidelity" and tries to persuade him to give up his mission in deference to love. The motivations for all these actions, as we shall see in a moment, are substantially different in *Polyeucte* from what they were in the *Aeneid*. Even on the level of plot, however, *Polyeucte* diverges in one very significant way from the *Aeneid*, and that is in its ending. In Vergil's poem the hero actually forsakes the woman, who out of shame and grief commits herself to the funeral pyre as her faithless lover is sailing off without her to found Rome. Polyeucte, on the other hand, though he leaves Pauline, does not forsake her. Because he refuses to renounce his Christian faith, he must suffer martyrdom;

but before he dies, he prays to God for his wife's conversion. And at the end of the play, after his own death, that prayer is answered. The Christian mission differs from the pagan mission in that it excludes no one from joining in. Aeneas never thinks—because Vergil never thought—that he could take Dido along with him on his journey. Corneille and Polyeucte see things otherwise; and the denouement is pointedly different.[4]

If we look at the play and the epic at other levels, we see similar patterns of convergence and divergence. Pauline, for example, resembles Dido in that both see themselves as victims of a lover's betrayal. In character or decorum, however, the women are virtual opposites. When Dido first hears of Aeneas's plan to leave Carthage, she explodes with raw fury:

> saevit inops animi totamque incensa per urbem
> bacchatur, qualis commotis excita sacris
> Thyias, ubi audito stimilant trieterica Baccho
> orgia nocturnusque vocat clamore Cithaeron.
>
> (ll. 300–303)[5]

> She rages through the city
> Like a woman mad, or drunk, the way the Maenads
> Go howling through the night-time on Cithaeron
> When Bacchus' cymbals summon with their clashing.
>
> (p. 97)[6]

Later she castigates Aeneas in a tirade of unmitigated verbal violence:

> nec tibi diva parens, generis nec Dardanus auctor,
> perfide, sed duris genuit te cautibus horrens
> Caucasus Hyrcanaeque admorunt ubera tigres.
>
> (ll. 365–67)

> You treacherous liar! No goddess was your mother,
> No Dardanus the founder of your tribe,
> Son of the stony mountain-crags, begotten
> On cruel rock, with a tigress for a wet-nurse!
>
> (p. 100)

Still later she vows eternal vengeance and begs the gods and the Furies to pursue her faithless lover with relentless torment:

> at bello audacis populi vexatus et armis,
> finibus extorris, complexu avolsus Iuli
> auxilium imploret videatque indigna suorum

funera; nec cum se sub leges pacis iniquae
tradiderit, regno aut optata luce fruatur,
sed cadat ante diem mediaque inhumatus harena.
haec precor, hanc vocem extremam cum sanguine fundo.
tum vos, o Tyrii, stirpem et genus omne futurum
exercete odiis cinerique haec mittite nostro
munera.

(ll. 615–24)

Let him be driven by arms and war, an exile,
Let him be taken from his son, Iulus,
Let him beg for aid, let him see his people dying
Unworthy deaths, let him accept surrender
On unfair terms, let him never enjoy the kingdom,
The hoped-for light, let him fall and die, untimely,
Let him lie unburied on the sand. Oh, hear me,
Hear the last prayer, poured out with my last blood!
And you, O Tyrians, hate, and hate forever
The Trojan stock. Offer my dust this homage.

(p. 109)

This magnificent passage may well have suggested to Corneille the imprecations of Camille in *Horace.* The emotional pitch and the rhetorical movement of the two speeches are very close; and if there is a significant difference, it lies only in the more controlled, more deliberate fury of Camille, whom Corneille shows *choosing* to act the role of fury to Horace. Nothing in any of the speeches of Pauline seems to echo any of Dido's feverish excesses, however. Indeed, Pauline is so very restrained in her response that, except for one thing, one might suspect that her restraint had no connection at all with the Vergilian text. Pauline's confidant, Stratonice, at one point sounds very much like Dido, however; and Pauline gently, but firmly, rebukes her. The exchange occurs when Stratonice comes in to report the scandalous act that Polyeucte has just committed during the temple ceremony:

PAULINE

Il est mort!

STRATONICE

Non, il vit; mais, ô pleurs superflus!
Ce courage si grand, cette âme si divine,
N'est plus digne du jour, ni digne de Pauline.
Ce n'est plus cet époux si charmant à vos yeux;

C'est l'ennemi commun de l'Etat et des Dieux,
Un méchant, un infâme, un rebelle, un perfide,
Un traître, un scélérat, un lâche, un parricide,
Une peste exécrable à tous les gens de bien,
Un sacrilège impie: en un mot, un chrétien.

PAULINE

Ce mot auroit suffi sans ce torrent d'injures.

STRATONICE

Ces titres aux chrétiens sont-ce des impostures?

PAULINE

Il est ce que tu dis, s'il embrasse leur foi;
Mais il est mon époux, et tu parles à moi.

(3. 2. 776–88)

The outburst of Stratonice links the play to the epic, and, doing so, allows us not just to see but to measure the distance separating Pauline from Dido. Pauline's moderation is so great in this scene that it verges on true Christian virtue. Unlike Dido, she expresses no desire at all for retaliation:

Apprends que mon devoir ne dépend point du sien:
Qu'il y manque, s'il veut; je dois faire le mien.

(3. 2. 795–96)

She is even careful to distinguish the man from the act:

Quelque chrétien qu'il soit, je n'en ai point d'horreur;
Je chéris sa personne, et je hais son erreur.

(3. 2. 799–800)

Dido's vituperation upon learning of Aeneas's betrayal is only one sign of her lack of self-control. Another, earlier manifestation was seen in her burning passion for the Trojan hero and her willingness to enter into a liaison with him. Pauline shows no such weakness. On the contrary, her behavior throughout the play never ceases to be absolutely correct. She is, of course, married to the hero, so that her love for him is always fully sanctioned. Her dealings with Sévère are no less proper. She agrees to see him only when her father forces her to do so; and she makes no effort to conceal her feelings about Sévère from Polyeucte. Her husband, as a consequence, far from being jealous, only admires his wife's nobility of character all the more.

These differences stand out with special clarity when they

are seen against the common ground of the two heroines' final resort to suicide or its prospect. Dido's self-immolation as Aeneas's ships are setting sail forms the magnificent conclusion to book 4 of the *Aeneid.* It restores dignity to the Carthaginian queen and makes up in part for her earlier loss of *pudor.* The parallel scene in *Polyeucte* occurs toward the end of act 4, after Polyeucte, in order to provide for his wife's happiness after his death, has commended her to the safe-keeping of Sévère. Left alone with Sévère, Pauline is quick to scotch any hopes her Roman suitor might have and rejects categorically any possibility of marriage to him after Polyeucte's death:

> Mais sachez qu'il n'est point de si cruel trépas
> Où d'un front assuré je ne porte mes pas,
> Qu'il n'est point aux enfers d'horreurs que je n'endure,
> Plutôt que de souiller une gloire si pure,
> Que d'épouser un homme, après son triste sort,
> Qui de quelque façon soit cause de sa mort.
>
> (4. 5. 1341−46)

At this point in the action, Pauline is somewhere between the pagan world and the Christian. Were she already a Christian, her contemplation of suicide would be accounted sinful. Since she remains a pagan, in spite of her virtually Christian trepidation as regards the fate of suicides in the afterworld, the force of her determination may still function, and indeed does function, to ennoble her in the eyes of the audience. It is significant, however, that whereas for Dido suicide was a means of restoring a lost *pudor,* for Pauline it would have served instead to forestall a threatened loss of *gloire.* If Pauline were to follow the example of Dido in the matter of suicide, it would only be in order to ensure not resembling her otherwise.[7] So, again, a point of overlap enables us to gauge the difference between the epic and the play and thus to note the degree of rectification.

The great confrontation scene of act 4, an echo of a similar encounter in book 4 of the *Aeneid,* offers a chance to see the distance that Corneille has put between Polyeucte and Aeneas. In the face of Dido's barrage of recriminations and insults, Aeneas maintains a steadfastly heroic composure. He is touched by the suffering that his departure is causing, but he does not show that he is touched: "ille Iovis monitis immota tenebat/lumina et obnixus curam sub corde premebat" (ll. 331–32); "Jove bade him keep/Affection from his eyes, and grief in his heart/With never a sign" (p. 98). Dido notes his impassiveness and interprets it as a sign of unfeeling: "num fletu ingemuit nostro? num lumina flexit?/num lacrimas victus dedit aut miseratus amantem est?" (ll. 369–70); "When I was weeping/Did he so much as sigh? Did he turn his eyes,/Ever so little, toward me? Did he break at all,/Or weep, or give his lover a word of pity?" (p. 100). Aeneas sighs, but only out of Dido's presence. Later, Dido's sister, Anna, comes to beg Aeneas at least to delay his departure. Once more the hero remains steadfast ("immotus"), impervious to pleas and tears: in a famous simile, the poet compares him to a mighty oak tree able to withstand the blast of the fiercest storm (ll. 441–49). From the outset Dido has characterized her faithless lover as cruel (ll. 308, 311); his lack of apparent emotion throughout only confirms her initial suspicions that he no longer has any interest in her.[8]

With Polyeucte it is quite pointedly different. Pauline opens the scene with a mild rebuke: "Vous n'avez point ici d'ennemi que vous-même," and proceeds to remind her husband, first, of his obligations, not to her, but to his forebears and his subjects. Having failed to dissuade him from his course by these more general appeals, she comes finally, like Dido, to reproach him for his infidelity to her: "Cruel, car il est temps que ma douleur éclate,/Et qu'un juste reproche accable une âme ingrate" (ll. 1235–36). Her reproaches, used only as a last resort, express her own sense of hurt and incomprehension more than any hatred of Polyeucte: "C'est donc là le dégoût qu'apporte l'hyménée?/Je te suis odieuse après m'être donnée!" (ll. 1251–52). Most important of all, Polyeucte reacts to this tenderness with a sigh and, eventually, tears:

POLYEUCTE

Hélas!

PAULINE

Que cet hélas a de peine à sortir!
Encor s'il marquoit un heureux repentir,
Que tout forcé qu'il est, j'y trouverois de charmes!
Mais courage, il s'émeut, je vois couler des larmes.

(4.3. 1253–56)

Polyeucte not only is moved; he shows he is moved by the tears he freely sheds. Polyeucte's God demands the first love: "Il ne faut rien aimer qu'après lui, qu'en lui-même" (l. 74); "Je vous aime,/Beaucoup moins que mon Dieu, mais bien plus que moi-même" (ll. 1279–80). He does not require, like Jove, that the hero stop up his ears to human suffering, however. Pauline does not, of course, succeed in deflecting Polyeucte from his purpose, but Polyeucte's tears are a sign to her that he has not ceased loving her and a promise that she need not, like Dido, be left behind. The sharp dichotomy seen in the *Aeneid*, where the hero conceals all of his emotions and the heroine none of hers, gives way in *Polyeucte* to a more evolved and temperate decorum shared by both lovers, a decorum that mitigates the pain of separation by affirming, on another level, the survival of their union: Pauline hates her husband's "error," not Polyeucte himself; Polyeucte accepts separation from his wife in this world, but prays for reunion with her in the next.

The other roles in the play may also be seen as part of a rectification of book 4 of the *Aeneid*. Néarque, for example, functions as the modern equivalent of Mercury, the divine messenger sent by Jove to warn Aeneas. Like his ancient counterpart, Néarque admonishes the hero not to neglect his mission for love of a woman, but rather to break away decisively and without further delay:

> tu nunc Karthaginis altae
> fundamenta locas pulchramque uxorius urbem
> extruis, heu, regni rerumque oblite tuarum?
> ipse deum tibi me claro demittit Olympo
> regnator, caelum et terras qui numine torquet,
> ipse haec ferre iubet celeris mondata per auras:
> quid struis, aut qua spe Libycis teris otia terris?
>
> (ll. 265–71)

> What are you doing,
> Forgetful of your kingdom and your fortunes,
> Building for Carthage? Woman-crazy fellow,
> The ruler of the gods, the great compeller
> Of heaven and earth, has sent me from Olympus
> With no more word than this: what are you doing,
> With what ambition [are you] wasting time in Libya?
>
> (p. 96)

Quoi? vous vous arrêtez aux songes d'une femme!
De si foibles sujets troublent cette grande âme!

(1. 1. 1–2)

Quoi? vous mêler aux voeux d'une troupe infidèle!
Oubliez-vous déjà que vous êtes chrétien?

(2. 6. 638–39)

non fugis hinc praeceps, dum praecipitare potestas?
. . . .
heia age, rumpe moras. varium et mutabile semper
femina.

(ll. 565–70)

Seize the moment
While it can still be seized, and hurry, hurry!
. . . .
Shove off, be gone! A shifty, fickle object
Is woman, always.

(p. 107)

. . . ce qu'on diffère est à demi rompu.
Rompez ses premiers coups [=ceux du diable] ; laissez pleurer
    Pauline.
Dieu ne veut point d'un coeur que le monde domine.

(1. 1. 64–66)

Hâtez-vous donc de l'être [=d'être chrétien].

(1. 1. 93)

        Fuyez.
            —Je ne puis.
            —Il le faut:
Fuyez un ennemi qui sait votre défaut.

(1. 1. 103–4)

Perhaps the major rectification regarding Néarque has to do
with the status of the messenger as compared with that of the
hero. In the *Aeneid*, the messenger is divine; the hero, mortal—a
traditional contrast that Tasso retains in the *Gerusalemme*,
where the messenger is the angel Gabriel. In *Polyeucte*, God
manifests himself and his truth by sending down to mankind,
not a god-like messenger with a specific message, but rather an
extraordinary capacity by which ordinary men may understand
God's message for themselves. This capacity, grace, figures
prominently in each of the two main scenes between Polyeucte

and Néarque. In act 1 Néarque argues that his friend has already received the grace of God, but stands in danger of losing it if he fails to act on it at once:

> . . . sa grâce
> Ne descend pas toujours avec même efficace;
> Le bras qui la versoit en devient plus avare,
> Et cette sainte ardeur qui doit porter au bien
> Tombe plus rarement, ou n'opère plus rien.
>
> (1. 1. 29–36)

In act 2, on the other hand, it is Polyeucte, fresh from baptism, who enjoys the purer state of grace. Consequently the new convert now begins to play the role of "messenger" himself and, in a curious reversal, enlightens Néarque just as, before, Néarque had enlightened him. In the *Aeneid* it would have been inappropriate for the hero to contradict Mercury and unthinkable for him to appear superior in any way. In *Polyeucte*, however, since all divinity is lodged in God and God's grace, it is natural that the hero should surpass his original, human mentor.[9]

In fact Polyeucte overrules his friend on another matter even before receiving the gift of baptismal grace. Like Mercury, Néarque takes a very dim view of women and consequently of love. In the *Aeneid* no countervailing argument is heard, from either the hero or the poet. Corneille, however, intends to save Pauline, and he lays the groundwork for her salvation in the very first scene of the play, where Polyeucte speaks up in defense both of his wife and of the legitimate pleasures of the conjugal bed:

> Mais vous ne savez pas ce que c'est qu'une femme:
> Ni le juste pouvoir qu'elle prend sur une âme,
> Quand après un long temps qu'elle a su nous charmer,
> Les flambeaux de l'hymen viennent de s'allumer.
>
> (1. 1. 9–12)

Though a Christian, Néarque seems to be clinging still to an earlier, pagan conception of love or to a conception of heroic mission that at least tends to exclude love for a woman. In the matter of love, Polyeucte knows more than Néarque from the outset; and this knowledge can be taken as another sign of Polyeucte's superiority.

The epic and the play alike focus primarily on the story of a hero who, at the instigation of some divine power, abandons a woman in order to fulfill his mission. The "rectified" couple exemplify a new, enhanced decorum; more tenderness, more understanding mark all their relations with each other, moderating the effect of the breach that opens up between them and preparing the way for their eventual reunion in the faith of Christ. The process of rectification extends beyond this central story, however, and embraces also a secondary story that revolves around the hero's rival. The rival in book 4 of the *Aeneid* is Iarbas, a neighboring king who is also the son of Jove. Vergil gives this role nowhere near the prominence that Corneille lends to the role of Sévère in *Polyeucte*; but the situations and themes are so close that one can see the derivation—and the accompanying rectification—very clearly, nevertheless. Iarbas figures four times in the action of book 4, usually as an unseen agent. At the beginning Anna mentions him as the most important of the various suitors whom Dido, before meeting Aeneas, had always rejected out of fidelity to the memory of her slain husband, Sychaeus (ll. 36–38). The next we hear of Iarbas is as a motivating force behind Aeneas's departure: for it is Iarbas who, angered by news of Dido's liaison with the Trojan hero, has complained to his father, Jove, thereby precipitating the dispatch of Mercury to warn Aeneas not to stay any longer in Carthage (ll. 195–218). The two remaining mentions of Iarbas both have to do with possible complications once Aeneas has left. Dido foresees either that Iarbas will do her harm out of a spirit of vengeance (ll. 325–26) or that she will have to agree to marry him (ll. 534–36). It is in part to avoid this very fate that she decides instead to commit suicide. The parallels with *Polyeucte* are not hard to see: both Iarbas and Sévère are rivals from the past who constitute some sort of threat for the present and future, particularly for the woman. Inside the framework of overall similarity, the differences are many and obvious, however. Aeneas and Iarbas never meet in the *Aeneid*; Polyeucte and Sévère not only do meet but come to admire and eventually to try to help one another, Polyeucte by offering Pauline to Sévère, Sévère by agreeing to intervene to save Polyeucte. More important, Sévère and Pauline confront each other on a much higher ethical plane than Iarbas and Dido, without loss to the play of any of the sense of danger associated, in the epic, with the rival's possible or likely retaliation.

Corneille accomplishes this rectification largely through the character of Félix.

When Pauline rejected Sévère and then married Polyeucte, she was not acting as a free agent, as Dido was when she refused Iarbas's offer of marriage and then entered into a liaison with Aeneas. Pauline had been totally dependent on her father; and it is thus Félix who, in the play, bears the responsibility for the affront to the rival. As a consequence, it is also he who most fears the rival's vengeance. Felix's dread of what might happen when Sévère learns of Pauline's marriage becomes a central theme and a key motive force in the play; and it is connected with the problem of reading Sévère's character for what it really is. Pauline has seen her former suitor in a dream, "la vengeance à la main" (1. 222); and Félix is panic-stricken upon learning of Sévère's approach: "Que ne permettra-t-il à son ressentiment?" (1. 324). Even Sévère's confidant, Fabian, tries to dissuade his friend from meeting with the married Pauline: "Vous vous échapperez sans doute en sa présence: / Un amant qui perd tout n'a plus de complaisance" (ll. 437–38). Pauline herself somewhat later expresses similar fears about how Sévère and Polyeucte may react when they confront each other in the temple ceremony: "Adieu: vous l'y verrez; pensez à son pouvoir, / Et vous resouvenez que sa faveur est grande" (ll. 632–33). These fears and these precautions all rest on the assumption that Sévère, the rejected suitor, may well resort to vengeance, may act, that is, more or less like Iarbas.

Pauline is not always so fearful as in the two instances cited above; and she tries to reassure her father at the outset that Sévère is "trop généreux" to think of taking vengeance. It is Polyeucte, however, who has the greatest faith in Sévère:

> Et je ne pense pas qu'on puisse avec raison
> D'un coeur tel que le sien craindre une trahison.
> . . . .
> Allez, tout son crédit n'a rien que j'appréhende;
> Et comme je connois sa générosité,
> Nous ne nous combattrons que de civilité.
>
> (2. 4–5. 603–4, 634–36)

The revelation of Sévère's true nobility of character and the confirmation of Polyeucte's faith in him come out in two key scenes with Pauline: during their first interview when, contrary to what Fabian predicted, Sévère does not "s'échapper" nor lose his sense of "complaisance"; then, later, during the scene in act 4, when Sévère not only relinquishes all hope of gaining Pauline for himself, but accedes to her plea that he try to save Polyeucte, his rival.

Félix, who witnesses neither of these interviews, persists in anticipating the worst of Sévère, however. "Il est homme, et sensible, et je l'ai dédaigné," he says to his confidant at the end of act 3, in a scene that represents, ethically speaking, the lowest point in the play's action:

> Et des mépris reçus son esprit indigné,
> Que met au désespoir cet hymen de Pauline,
> Du courroux de Décie obtiendroit ma ruine.
> Pour venger un affront tout semble être permis,
> Et les occasions tentent les plus remis.
>
> (3. 5. 1035–40)

And he reiterates these fears later on, just before the catastrophe:

> Peut-être dès demain, dès la nuit, dès ce soir,
> J'en verrois des effets que je ne veux pas voir;
> Et Sévère aussitôt, courant à sa vengeance,
> M'iroit calomnier de quelque intelligence.
> Il faut rompre ce coup, qui me seroit fatal.
>
> (5. 1. 1497–1501)

In the *Aeneid* it is Iarbas's complaint to Jove, king of the gods, that undoes the happiness of Dido. Sévère does not in fact appeal for redress to the emperor Décie; but Félix is afraid that he might, and that fear alone suffices to precipitate the tragedy. Just as *Rodogune* preserves the death of the mother—common both to the historical incident and to the Electra legend—while freeing the son of any blame, so here in *Polyeucte* the end point of the action in book 4 of the *Aeneid*—the separation of the lovers—remains intact, but the "acheminements" leading up to it have undergone a radical change that frees not only the hero but the heroine and the rival also from any blame. Sévère lives up to his hard-sounding name (and resembles his Vergilian counterpart) only once in the play, when he explodes in anger at Félix for not having believed his professions of good faith and for having sent Polyeucte accordingly to his death:

La faveur que pour lui je vous avois offerte,
Au lieu de le sauver, précipite sa perte!
J'ai prié, menacé, mais sans vous émouvoir;
Et vous m'avez cru fourbe ou de peu de pouvoir!
Eh bien! à vos dépens vous saurez que Sévère
Ne se vante jamais que de ce qu'il peut faire;
Et par votre ruine il vous fera juger
Que qui peut bien vous perdre eût pu vous protéger.

(5. 6. 1751–58)

Without the obtuseness of Félix, the play could not end as it does with a catastrophe for which none of the three principal heroes need bear responsibility. Félix is clearly a scapegoat figure and, just as clearly, an essential element in the play's rectification of the *Aeneid.* It is perhaps in secret recognition of this character's usefulness that Corneille finally "saves" Félix too—through a conversion to the Christian faith that effectively releases him from the threat spoken above by Sévère.[10]

Polyeucte, in conclusion, is clearly an unacknowledged (that is, hidden) rectification of book 4 of the *Aeneid.* All the major characters, all the important incidents serve to link the play to Vergil's epic and, at the same time, delineate significant differences between the two works. It remains to be seen, in the next chapter, why Corneille chose to modernize the Vergilian text in this fashion.

CHAPTER III
Polyeucte: Vergil and Tasso

TO INDICATE THE PRESENCE OF RECTIFICATION, AS I attempted to do in the previous chapter, is not, of course, to explain it. For explanation, one has to seek answers to two questions: What motivated the poet's decision to work with a particular text; and what motivated the particular means by which he chose to "rectify" it? In the case of the little tragedy in *L'Illusion comique*, one can suppose that Corneille chose to revise elements of the story of Medea because he had just come from writing *Médée*. The story was fresh in his mind, and it would be natural for him to be interested in exploring other dramatic possibilities that might be found in the material. One can posit also that the playwright transposed the Medea story to a vaguely modern setting (or perhaps to a neutral setting, one at least that is not presented as ancient), in order to bring the action closer to the audience's normal frame of reference (as he had done in two of his comedies, for example, by setting them forthrightly in Paris). To this, one would have to add that the little tragedy in act 5 is only a small part of a more complex work that altogether constitutes both a summary of the playwright's own past achievements and a manifesto expressing the poet's faith in the theater and in his own talent. Concerning *Polyeucte*, one might cite the prestige of Vergil, the *Aeneid*, and its famous lovers as possible reasons for Corneille to have been drawn to the subject. And the hidden rectification of *Médée* in *L'Illusion comique* could serve as precedent for transposing the material borrowed from Vergil. Why the playwright should have chosen to situate the Vergilian story in a Christian, hagiographical setting is less easy to understand, however. Corneille was a devout Christian; and there had been a few (though not many) plays with religious themes on the profane stage, that is, outside the *collèges*, where, on the contrary, the genre flourished.[1] But in adapting *Le Cid*, he had taken care to excise all the specifically Christian elements found in the work of Guillén de Castro. The Christian subject of *Polyeucte* represents a deliberate reversal, then, of the poet's earlier attitude toward treating religion on the stage; and the reason for this reversal is not immediately apparent. This question, as well as several others, is clarified, however, if we examine *Polyeucte* and its rectification of Vergil in the context of the Quarrel of the *Cid* and its consequences.

The theory of rectification as the seventeenth century understood it rests, as we have seen, on the dual assumption that the poet is always free to alter history but morally bound to alter it only for the better. In the *Cid* Corneille had erred in retaining intact certain offensive elements inherited from history; but Scudéry had also been at fault, in a different way, when he claimed that the poet could not change historical fact. Chapelain believed that out of literary contention one could sometimes gain a clearer insight into the mysteries of poetical creation. The theory of rectification constitutes one of the key dialectical discoveries of the *Sentiments*, and Chapelain presents it in the form of a double response to Scudéry and Corneille. Because he views criticism, like literature, as a continuing development in history, he invokes the example of earlier poetical practice and earlier critical response in adumbrating his own modern theory. Though, as we saw earlier, he cites both Vergil and Tasso as authorities, it is Vergil and book 4 of the *Aeneid* that figure most prominently in the critic's thought at this point.

Chapelain begins by recalling the fact, well known in literary history at the time, that Vergil had radically altered historical fact in recounting the story of Dido and Aeneas:

> Le Poëte ne considere dans l'histoire que la vray-semblance des evenemens, sans se rendre esclave des circonstances qui en accompagnent la verité. De maniere que pourveu qu'il soit vray-semblable que plusieurs actions se soient aussi bien peu faire conjointement que separément, il est libre au Poëte de les rapprocher, si par ce moyen il peut rendre son Ouvrage plus merveilleux. Il ne faut point d'autre preuve de cette doctrine que l'exemple de Virgile dans sa Didon, qui selon tous

les Chronologistes nasquit plus de deux cens ans apres Enée;
si l'on ne veut encore adjouster celuy du Tasse dans le Renaud
de sa Hierusalem, lequel ne pouvoit estre né qu'à peine, lors
que mourut Godefroy de Bouïllon.   (Gasté, p. 371)

The two-hundred-year discrepancy mentioned by Chapelain
may be exaggerated. In any event, the historical figures of Dido
and Aeneas did live in different times and could never in fact
have known each other. Moreover, though the real Dido had
indeed founded Carthage, she had killed herself only to honor a
commitment to the memory of Sychaeus, her husband, and to
avoid a forced marriage to Iarbas. Vergil probably chose Dido as
his heroine because he wanted to include within his poem some
kind of explanation for the age-old hostility between Rome and
Carthage; then, once he had chosen her, he remodeled the character along the lines of earlier literary heroines like Calypso,
Nausicaä, and especially Medea, all of whom function as obstacles of foreign extraction impeding the progress of the hero toward his rightful goal (Pease, ed., *Aeneidos Liber Quartus*, pp.
12–14). For all we know, Vergil may in fact have started with a
literary model and then sought some kind of historical equivalent. Through the ages, however, critics have tended to assume
the opposite and, as Chapelain does, have stressed the changes
made in the historical sources of the poem.

Most readers of the *Aeneid*, one must assume, never ques-
tioned Vergil's procedures in book 4, even if they knew enough
to be aware of them. They simply gave themselves over to the
beauty and poetic truth of the story, like Macrobius, who said:
"Indeed, the beauty of Vergil's narrative has so far prevailed that,
although all are aware of the Phoenician queen and know that
she laid hands on herself to save her good name, still they turn a
blind eye to the fiction, suppress in their minds the evidence of
the truth, and choose rather to regard as true the tale which the
charm of a poet's imagination has inplanted in the heart of mankind" (*Saturnalia*, 5. 17. 6). Others, however, were not so quick
as Macrobius to excuse Vergil. Several Christian writers from
Africa—Tertullian, Minucius Felix, and Jerome in particular—
were disturbed that Vergil had sullied the reputation of a chaste
queen; and from the protestations of these critics emerged in
time the tradition of a chaste, historical Dido alongside that of

the unchaste, Vergilian Dido. Boccaccio, Petrarch, Buchanan, and others had kept alive the memory of an innocent Dido in the modern era, so much so that in 1641, only a few years after the Quarrel, Boisrobert wrote a play called *La Vraye Didon ou la Didon chaste*, perhaps intended to counterbalance the Vergilian *Didon* of Scudéry that had been published in 1637, when the Quarrel over the *Cid* was still raging.[2]

The ongoing debate over the two Didos contained, in any event, all the elements necessary to formulate the theory of rectification; it remained only to set them in the proper relationship to each other, which is what Chapelain accomplished in the following page from the *Sentiments*:

> Ainsi l'Observateur, selon nostre avis, ne conclut pas bien quant il dit, *que le Cid n'est pas un bon sujet de Poëme Dramatique, pour ce qu'estant historique, et par consequent veritable, il ne pouvoit estre changé, ny rendu propre au theatre*, d'autant que si Virgile par exemple a bien fait d'une honneste femme une femme impudique, sans qu'il fust necessaire, il auroit bien peu estre permis à un autre de faire pour l'utilité publique d'un mariage extravagant un qui fust raisonnable; en y apportant les ajustemens, et y prenant les bihais qui en pouvoient corriger les defauts.   (Gasté, p. 368)

Chapelain stops short of joining those who blame Vergil, on moral grounds, for having traduced Dido, but he makes it clear that nowadays a poet would be well advised to strive to achieve the highest decorum possible:

> Nous sçavons bien que quelques-uns ont blasmé Virgile d'en avoir usé de la sorte, mais outre que nous doutons si l'opinion de ces Censeurs est recevable, et s'ils connoissoient autant que luy jusqu'où s'estend la juridiction de la Poësie, nous croyons encore que s'ils l'ont blasmé ce n'a pas esté d'avoir simplement alteré l'histoire, mais de l'avoir alteré de bien en mal; de maniere qu'ils ne l'ont pas accusé proprement d'avoir peché contre l'Art en changeant la verité, mais contre les bonnes moeurs en diffamant une personne, qui avoit mieux aymé mourir que de vivre diffamée. Il en fust arrivé tout au contraire dans le changement qu'on eust peu faire au sujet du Cid puis qu'on eust corrigé les mauvaises moeurs qui se trouvent dans l'histoire, et qu'on les eust rendües bonnes par la Poësie pour l'utilité du Public.   (Gasté, pp. 368–69)

Elsewhere, at the close of the *Sentiments*, as we have already seen, Chapelain says that poets and critics alike must be judged, in part, in relation to the time in which they lived. Flaws that only since have come to be perceived as such remain flaws, but cannot in justice be held against earlier poets; modern poets, however, must beware of imitating what they, now, should be able to recognize clearly as flaws.[3] The implication for Corneille was clear: the enthusiastic acceptance of the *Cid* by persons of literary sensitivity and good taste suggested that it, like the *Aeneid*, was a poem containing, along with some possible flaws, a store of genuine poetic truth and beauty. Profiting from the controversy occasioned by the attacks on the *Cid*, Corneille easily could, and obviously should, take steps in the future to avoid the kind of flaws that had marred the *Cid*. He had not, like Vergil, gone so far as to invent his heroine's shortcomings; he had only kept a shocking marriage provided by history. But he could employ the poet's right to invent, a right guaranteed in the *Aeneid*, to go even further and to *improve* upon history. The requirement that action be *bienséante* as well as *vraisemblable* was in the nature of a newly emerged (or emerging) rule for the poet; it was a way of reconciling the various demands of poetry and morality, a means of pleasing both the ardent admirers of Vergil (like Macrobius) and the dissenters on ethical grounds (like Tertullian and Jerome). Corneille, in short, was being urged to keep the dramatic effectiveness achieved in the *Cid* while adding to it a stricter, more appropriate heroic decorum.

Polyeucte fulfils just such a purpose. More than that, it shows that it is fulfilling that purpose by revising the very materials of book 4 of the *Aeneid*. The play in effect combines the traditions of the two Didos and gives us a chaste Dido who nevertheless meets and falls in love with, and marries, her Aeneas. If Vergil had done the same, Tertullian and Jerome would have joined Macrobius in unstinted praise of the *Aeneid*. By this combination of the two Didos, Corneille, for his part, stood to silence the critics of the *Cid* and perhaps win the ultimate prize of universal acclaim. The point where *Polyeucte* most obviously reflects the Quarrel and the *Sentiments* in particular would appear to be the scene in act 4 where Pauline rejects the idea of marriage to Sévère after the death of Polyeucte. This situation is the exact parallel of the situation in which the real, chaste Dido found herself; but Corneille has so beautifully meshed the historical chaste Dido with the corrected Dido derived from Vergil that one cannot detect any difference at all between the two. On the other hand, Pauline's very strict sense of propriety is in clear contrast to Chimène's (to some) shocking hesitations at the end of the *Cid*. The new heroine, far from yielding to temptation, as Corneille's critics said Chimène was guilty of doing, takes a position of the utmost severity and refuses a marriage that even her husband has tried to urge upon her. *Polyeucte* acts, then, to correct the *Cid* by means of rectifying book 4 of the *Aeneid*.

The idea was not, of course, to cast blame on Vergil. If such had been the playwright's aim, he obviously would not have concealed the rectification as he does. The point was to join the march of poetry through history as deliberately as possible, to exploit what was best in the poetic tradition handed down from antiquity, to learn from past errors and even perhaps to profit from the storm over the *Cid*, so that eventually one might add significantly to the treasury of great poetry available to man. Other great poets of the past might have been able to help Corneille to this goal just as well as Vergil. But by general consensus, Vergil was the geatest poet who had ever lived. The fact that the greatest epic poem of all time had, by coincidence, raised some of the same sorts of criticism as those leveled against the *Cid* made it natural that Corneille would pay special attention, after the *Sentiments*, to book 4 of the *Aeneid*. The decision to rectify the story of Dido and Aeneas itself, however, implies not just a desire to advance beyond the *Cid*, but a firm determination on the part of the playwright to impose upon himself in the process the most stringent of theoretical exigencies conceivable.

There remains the related question of why Corneille decided to retell the Vergilian story through the life of a Christian saint. Though Chapelain laid on the poet the obligation to make changes only for the better, nowhere did he advise Christian themes or even explicitly Christian standards of behavior. He did, as we have seen, encourage Corneille to ponder certain of the lessons of Tasso's career, however; and if Corneille acted on this advice and turned to Tasso, particularly to the *Discorsi*, as seems likely, he would have found there in the theory of the successor to Vergil a magnificent supplement to the *Sentiments*—a grander, bolder, more poetic, and more imaginative articulation of Chapelain's most cherished ideas, a modern poetics of unquestioned authority.

The *Discorsi* is in fact two fairly substantially different works. The *Discorsi dell'arte poetica*, written perhaps as early as 1561–62 but not published until 1587 (six years after the *Gerusalemme*) contains three books devoted one each to the invention, disposition, and poetic ornamentation of heroic subjects. The *Discorsi del poema eroico* of 1594, on the other hand, is an expansion of the earlier work and, among other things, an attempt to answer critics of the *Gerusalemme*. Not much has been changed from the youthful version, but a great deal has been added: an introductory chapter, lengthy passages in the sections on invention and disposition (now books 2 and 3) and a much fuller treatment of elocution in three books rather than the original one. The shorter work has the advantage of greater coherence, but the mature richness of Tasso's thought in the *Discorsi del poema eroico* makes the later work more valuable. In 1639 Jean Baudoin translated and appended to the end of his *Recueil d'emblemes divers* (pp. 577–619) a short text of Tasso's entitled, rather misleadingly, "Du poëme heroique": it is in reality only book 1 of the *Discorsi dell'arte poetica*, on the invention or discovery of heroic subjects for poetry. Italian versions of one or the other of the *Discorsi* were available, however; and, if he did not already own a copy, Corneille would have had no trouble finding one to buy or borrow. In what follows I shall refer to the expanded treatise, the *Discorsi del poema eroico*, as edited by Poma.

Tasso's remarks on the choice of a properly heroic subject are predicated on two main assumptions: the poet must be free to manipulate his material so as to produce the desired aesthetic effect; and he must aim at the marvelous without loss of verisimilitude. The subject, to begin with, must be exceptionally illustrious (p. 101). Inasmuch as it is improbable that great noble deeds should have gone unnoticed and unrecorded, the poet ought to draw his subject from history (p. 84), and more specifically from an era neither so recent as to inhibit his freedom to introduce changes nor so remote as to seem excessively alien to the audience (pp. 98–99). The subject should also be based on true religion. True religion, for one thing, serves to rationalize the marvelous, which is indispensable. Religious subjects of a sacred nature, however, cannot be modified in any way and therefore should be avoided (pp. 93, 98). Love, provided it is noble and not base, is very appropriate (pp. 104–8). And though tragic heroes must have a flaw, epic heroes represent, and must embody, the highest virtues conceivable; in the modern era, epic heroes must therefore necessarily be Christian: "Laonde proporrei de gran lunga la persona di Carlo e d'Artu a quella di Teseo e di Giasone" (p. 98). These requirements are obviously designed to fit and to justify the *Gerusalemme* in particular; except for the matter of the tragic hero's having to have a tragic flaw, they also apply very well to *Polyeucte*, however, even though the time-frame in the play is Christian Rome rather than the Middle Ages.

Tasso includes much more than practical advice about choosing a subject, however; in books 2 and 3 he develops, rather at random but still quite clearly, a fully articulated theory of literary history that sets the modern poet into meaningful relationship with the greatest poets of antiquity. Thus, in the process of refuting the idea that romance, a new form, is essentially different from epic poetry—a burning question in the debate of the *Gerusalemme* versus the *Orlando furioso*[4]—Tasso is at pains to distinguish between those poetic elements, such as the unity of the fable, that he deems constant generic requirements, and other elements, including decorum especially, that are subject to change:

> È la natura stabilissima nelle sue operazioni, e procede sempre con un tenore certo e perpetuo (se non quanto per difetto e inconstanza della materia si vede talor variare), perché, guidata da un lume e da una scorta infallibile, riguarda sempre il buono e 'l perfetto; ed essendo il buono e 'l perfetto sempre il medesimo, conviene che 'l suo modo di operare sia sempre l'istesso. Opera della natura è la bellezza, la qual consistendo in certa proporzion di membra con grandezza convenevole e con vaga soavità di colori, queste condizioni, che belle per se stesse una volta furono, belle sempre saranno, né potrebbe l'uso fare ch'altrimente paressero; sì come all'incontra non può far l'uso sì che belli paiano i capi aguzzi o i gosi fra quelle nazioni ove si veggiano nella maggior parte degli uomini e delle donne . . . Laonde ragionevolmente da Cicerone nella

Topica la natura e l'arte sono annoverate fra le cagioni le quali hanno costanza, perché non sogliono variare i loro effetti. . . . (pp. 135–36)

Le cose poi, che dall'usanza dependono, come la maniera dell'armeggiare, i modi dell'avventure, i costumi de' sacrifici e de' conviti, le cerimonie, il decoro e la maestà delle persone, queste, dico, come piace all'usanza che oggi vive e signoreggia il mondo, si possono accomodare. (p. 136)

It would be inappropriate today, Tasso says, for the daughter of a king to go to wash clothes in the river like Nausicaä; and Trissino was rightly blamed for imitating Homer in things that changing custom has rendered less praiseworthy.

Notable among those things, besides unity, that Tasso tends to view as constants are poetic talent (in the sense that it can occur in its absolute fullness in any age) and such basic genres as epic poetry and tragedy. There is a very brief passage that might be construed as leaving the door open, not to the creation of new genres, but at least to the emergence of permutations hitherto neglected (p. 132). On the whole, however, Tasso is very conservative as to genres; and he repeats several times the idea that epic and tragedy are differentiated both by their modes (one being narrated, the other represented) and also by their subject matters (epic with a perfect, tragedy with a flawed, hero). The question of high poetic competence he discusses in relation to two non-artistic factors that define and, in certain ages, limit it to some extent:

Replicherò in questo luogo quel che altre volte ho detto, cioè che l'eccellentissimo poema è proprio solamente della eccellentissima forma di governo. Questa è il regno; ma il regno non può esser ottimamente governato con falsa religione. Conviene adunque all'ottimo regno la vera religione; e ove sia falsa pietà e falso culto d'Iddio, non può essere alcuna perfezione nel principe o nel principato. Però i poemi ancora participano dell'istessa imperfezione; ma il difetto non è dell'arte poetica, ma della politica, non del poeta, ma de' legislatori. (p. 95)

This important distinction allows Tasso to praise Homer and Vergil as supreme poets at the same time that he notes the presence in their poems of certain imperfections deriving from the times in which the poets lived. We have seen much this same combination of veneration for the Ancients and recognition of their necessary limitations elsewhere, in the *Sentiments* of Chapelain: "Ceux qui viennent apres [les Anciens] heritent bien de leurs richesses, mais non pas de leurs privileges, et les vices d'Euripide ou de Seneque ne sçauroient faire approuver ceux de Guillen de Castro." The job of the poet, as Tasso sees it, is to cling to what is true and valid in the works of the Ancients but to change what is outmoded or discredited: "In questa parte non fu lodato il Trissino, ch'imitò in Omero quelle cose ancora che avea rendute men lodevoli la mutazione de' costumi" (p. 137).

If certain things remain constant in poetry, other things change, then; and the history of poetry is in large part an evolutionary process, in which Vergil or the *Aeneid* appears as the intermediary stage between the very archaic and the modern. On the matter of variety of incident, for example, a central theme in the debate over the relative merits of Ariosto and Tasso, Tasso adopts a moderately modernistic stance:

> Non era per aventura così necessaria questa varietà a'tempi di Virgilio e d'Omero, essendo gli uomini di quel secolo di gusto non così isvogliato; però non tanto v'attesero; maggiore nondimeno in Virgilio che in Omero si ritrova. Gratissima era a' nostri tempi, e perciò devevano i nostri poeti co' sapori di questa varietà condire i loro poemi, volendo che da questi gusti sì delicati non fossero schivati. . . . (p. 139)

The only check to this increasing emphasis on variety of incident is the absolute requirement, never subject to changing taste, that a poem, however numerous its episodes, must still show a clear unity of structure: "ma che nondimeno uno sia il poema che tanta varietà di materie contegna, una la forma e l'anima sua . . . " (p. 140). Of more interest to a student of *Polyeucte*, however, are a series of remarks concerning evolving heroic decorum in epic heroes. Aeneas, Tasso points out, is shown to bear intense physical pain (from a leg wound) with much greater fortitude and restraint than such earlier heroes as Hercules and Prometheus, who moan and groan at great length. Since a minor character of the *Iliad*, Eurypylus, is said to have resembled Aeneas in this respect, the sense of evolution in the hero's behavior is somewhat blurred, however (pp. 151–52).

More to the point is an extended passage in book 3 dealing with the moral aspects of the ending of the *Aeneid,* in which Aeneas ignores Turnus's pleas for mercy and runs him through with a sword. This passage of the *Discorsi,* known commonly as the "Difesa di Virgilio," was accidentally dropped by the printer, so that Corneille could not have read Tasso's conclusion, which exonerates Vergil on the grounds that he lived before the time of Christ and, in any event, represented, on this score, a marked improvement over Homer: "Giusta fu dunque la vendetta e lecita al cavaliero gentile (il quale non può esser riputato crudele da' gentili, o in comparazione degli altri), e molto più convenevole che la vendetta fatta d'Achille" (p. 160). The beginning of this comparison, which was not dropped, makes it clear enough, however, that Tasso viewed Aeneas as, on moral grounds, a superior epic hero to Achilles: "Ma Virgilio, se non m'inganno, vide meglio il decoro generale, perché formò in Enea la pietà, la religione, la continenza, la fortezza, la magnanimità, la giustizia e ciascun'altra virtù di cavaliero; e in questo particolare il fece maggiore del fero Achille . . . " (p. 156).

Another transformation that interests Tasso has to do with love, the theme of which he sees growing steadily in importance from Homer to Vergil to modern writers of epic and romance. Not only, however, does the sheer amount of attention paid to the amorous emotion change over time, so also does the nature of love itself. In the beginning men viewed love as little more than concupiscence and so subordinated it to the irascible faculty and to reason. Given the frame of reference, it is understandable that Homer should have taken wrath as his theme rather than love. As Saint Thomas has since shown—thus refuting Plato—there exists, however, a higher, nobler love that is not an appetite but a function of the will. This love, Tasso maintains, has in fact superseded wrath as the most appropriate, most praiseworthy of all heroic virtues: "Ma gli antichi o non conobbero questo amore, o non volsero descriverlo ne gli eroi; ma se non onorarono l'amore come virtù umana, l'adorarono quasi divina; però, niuna altra dovevano stimar più, conveniente a gli eroi. Laonde azioni eroiche ci potranno parer, oltre l'altre, quelle che son fatte per amore" (p. 106). This new type of love includes, but is not restricted to, the love that martyrs show for Christ: "Ma i poeti moderni, se non vogliono descriver la divinità dell'amore in quelli ch'espongono la vita per Cristo, possono ancora, nel formarvi un cavaliere, descriverci l'amore come un abito costante della volontà . . . " (p. 106). Tasso makes no overt reference to the *Gerusalemme liberata*, but his remarks on the *Iliad* and the *Aeneid* clearly serve to account for his own poem, both in its resemblance to its two earlier models and also in its *differentiae*. The basic rules of the epic genre are unchanging, and Tasso obviously is not going to claim a higher degree of poetic skill than Vergil or Homer possessed. Coming after them, being a poet of the Christian era, however, he carries with him the advantage of knowing, as his predecessors could not, what the true religion and what the highest virtues are. Though Paolo Beni, extrapolating still further, will reach the conclusion that the *Gerusalemme* therefore is a greater poem than either the *Aeneid* or the *Iliad*, Tasso himself does not transgress the bounds of modesty.[5] Nevertheless the *Discorsi*, especially in its expanded version, is clearly an apology for the *Gerusalemme*, or at least for the kind of epic that Tasso wrote in the *Gerusalemme*.

The view of literary history that emerges from the *Discorsi* involves more than rectification as understood by Chapelain. Vergil, as Tasso saw it, understood heroic decorum better than Homer, just as he himself, as a Christian poet, saw truths that even Vergil had failed to grasp. Yet he does not speak of one poet's "correcting" the imperfections or deficiencies of another. He sees poets as belonging to their age and each age as perceiving certain truths with less or more clarity. There is in the *Discorsi* a strong sense of cultural or ethical or religious evolution or progress; and this movement carries with it whole peoples, including their greatest poets. Chapelain's argument for rectification suffers from being at once too specific (too tied to the particular flaws of the *Cid*) and too abstract (too random and too vague as to its mode of operation and its ultimate justification). Tasso's view, more comprehensive and far nobler in conception, proposes, in place of mere rectification, the magnificent image of the world's greatest poets *succeeding* one another across the ages, each one doing all that it is possible to do in his own time.

Polyeucte conforms almost perfectly with Tasso's prescriptions for heroic poetry and in several ways seems even to echo passages in the *Discorsi*. Corneille had received permission to dedicate the play to Louis XIII; when the king died, the playwright addressed his dedicatory letter instead to Anne of Austria, Louis's widow. It was the first and only time in his long career that Corneille dedicated a work to a monarch. (The *Imitation de Jésus-Christ* would be dedicated, however, to the pope, Alexander VII.) The queen's piety and her exalted position set her quite apart, in Corneille's mind, from all other mortals; only the Christian subject matter of *Polyeucte* justified his desire to seek for it the royal protection:

> Toutes les fois que j'ai mis sur notre scène des vertus morales ou politiques, j'en ai toujours cru les tableaux trop peu dignes de paroître devant [Votre Majesté]. . . . Pour rendre les choses proportionnées, il failloit aller à la plus haute espèce, et n'entreprendre pas de rien offrir de cette nature à une reine très-chrétienne . . . à moins que de lui offrir un portrait des vertus chrétiennes dont l'amour et la gloire de Dieu formassent les plus beaux traits, et qui rendit les plaisirs qu'elle y pourra prendre aussi propres à exercer sa piété qu'à délasser son esprit. (*Oeuvres,* 3:472)

The most illustrious themes for heroic poetry, Tasso thought, must necessarily involve Christianity; and the ideal conditions for the heroic poet included living under a Christian monarch (p. 95). *Polyeucte*'s Christian subject and the playwright's dedication of the work to the queen thus realize the fundamental aims of the *Discorsi.*

In the Examen, Corneille points out, moreover, that he took care in selecting the subject of *Polyeucte* not to restrict the poet's prerogative to introduce changes: "Je me suis donné des licences que [Heinsius, Grotius, et Buchanan] n'ont pas prises, de changer l'histoire en quelque chose, et d'y mêler des épisodes d'invention" (*Oeuvres* 3:480). The fact that their subjects had been biblical and his merely hagiographical explains and justifies the different procedures because "nous ne devons qu'une croyance pieuse à la vie des saints, et nous avons le même droit sur ce que nous en tirons pour le porter au théâtre, que sur ce que nous empruntons des autres histoires; mais nous devons une foi chrétienne et indispensable à tout ce qui est dans la Bible, qui ne nous laisse aucune liberté d'y rien changer." Tasso had made the same distinction that Corneille makes here, and for the same purposes: "Ma l'istorie e le scritture sono sacre o non sacre; e delle sacre alcune hanno maggiore, altre minore

autorità; maggior autorità hanno l'ecclesiastiche e le spirituali.
. . . Nelle istorie [di questa] qualità a pena ardisca il poeta di
stender la mano . . . " (p. 98). Similarly, just as Tasso says in the
Discorsi that true religion serves to guarantee the credibility of
certain marvelous events in the poem (p. 93), so Corneille argues in the Examen that, in the Christian context of his play, the
sudden conversions of Pauline and Félix at the end do not transgress the limits of verisimilitude: "Félix . . . se convertit après
[Pauline]; et ces deux conversions, quoique miraculeuses, sont
si ordinaires dans les martyres, qu'elles ne sortent point de la
vraisemblance, parce qu'elles ne sont pas de ces événements
rares et singuliers qu'on ne peut tirer en exemple. . . . "

We have seen how the decorum of the three heroic
characters—Polyeucte, Pauline, and Sévère—represents a conscious (and concealed) rectification of the decorum of Aeneas,
Dido, and Iarbas in the *Aeneid*. This bears an obvious analogous
relationship to the differences that Tasso notes between the ferocity of Achilles and the relative mildness of Aeneas or between
the importance of love in ancient and modern epic poems. More
specifically, we can see that *Polyeucte* stresses love in two important ways specified by Tasso in the *Discorsi*. Tasso says that
the modern poet may content himself with depicting the new,
noble form of love as it is exemplified in "un cavaliere," but its
most sublime manifestation is found in the love that impels a
man to risk his life for Christ (p. 106). Corneille, in the person of
Polyeucte, combines as it were the knight and the martyr, thus
achieving the very highest stage of heroic virtue. Tasso, in com-
menting on the greater role given by Vergil to the theme of love
as compared with what one finds in the *Iliad*, goes on to note
that, even so, the *Aeneid* gives scant treatment to several amorous situations and characters that modern poets would be sure
to exploit more fully. Vergil, he says, has been blamed by some
for having feigned the love of Dido and Aeneas (thus besmirch-
ing the queen's reputation): "Parea nondimeno a costoro che
Vergilio fosse stato più ristretto e parco che non siamo noi altri,
perché molte cose e' poteva dire dell'amor d'Enea, molte di
quello d'Iarba, molte di quello di Turno e di Lavinia, le quali da
lui sono taciute o a pena accennate" (p. 104). The role of Sévère-
Iarbas quite clearly agrees with Tasso's conception of how a
modern poet would recreate book 4 of the *Aeneid*.

There is, however, one very important point on which *Polyeucte* is not in agreement with the *Discorsi.* According to Tasso it is the epic hero who must needs be Christian, and, ideally, a martyr in order to illustrate and embody the modern world's highest conception of virtue; the tragic hero, when he is mentioned, is said to be essentially different in that he is not perfect but flawed. Such, Tasso held, were the natural rules of the two genres of epic and tragic poetry:

> Richiede la tragedia persone né buone né cattive, ma d'una condizione di mezzo: tale è Oreste, Elettra, Giocasta, Eteocle, Edippo la cui persona fu da Aristotele giudicata attissima alla favola tragica. L'epico all'incontro vuole il sommo delle virtù; però le persone sono eroiche come è la virtù. Si ritrova in Enea l'eccellenza della pietà, della fortezza militare in Achille, della prudenza in Ulisse. (pp. 102–3)

> Ma quell'illustre ch'abbiamo detto esser proprio dell'eroico, può esser più o meno illustre: quanto la materia conterrà in sé avenimenti più nobili e più grandi, tanto sarà più disposta all'eccellentissima forma dell'epopeia. (p. 103)

> Imitano il romanzo e l'epopeia le medesime azioni, cioè l'illustri; né solo è fra loro quella convenienza, d'imitar l'illustri in genere, che è fra l'epico e 'l tragico, ma ancora una più particolare e più stretta d'imitare il medesimo illustre: quello, dico, che non è fondato sovra la grandezza de' fatti orribili e compassionevoli, ma sovra le generose e magnanime azioni degli eroi, e non si determina con le persone di mezzo fra 'l vizio e la virtù, ma elegge le valorose in supremo grado di eccellenza. . . . (p. 130)

Polyeucte is obviously conceived, in the manner of Achilles and Aeneas, as a hero in whom virtue shines forth with unadulterated, sublime power and beauty. He is an epic hero, not a tragic hero of middling goodness, like Oedipus or Orestes. Corneille's remarks on the perfect character of his hero could be—and probably are—directed above all at Tasso in the *Discorsi:* "Ceux qui veulent arrêter nos héros dans une médiocre bonté, où quelques interprètes d'Aristote bornent leur vertu, ne trouveront pas ici leur compte, puisque celle de Polyeucte va jusqu'à la sainteté, et n'a aucun mélange de foiblesse" (Examen).

There are other *differentiae* of the epic that Corneille, for the present, leaves alone: namely, the depiction of a group of wicked persons opposed to a group of virtuous heroes and the ensuing double reversal, whereby the wicked go from good to bad fortune and the virtuous from bad to good; and the arousal, not of pity and fear, but *admiration.* These, as we shall see, will come in time with *La Mort de Pompée* and *Nicomède.* Félix, though he serves much the same narratological function as the evil characters of the modern epic, is not in fact wicked; and his conversion spares him, as we have seen, an imminent fall from "good" to "bad" fortune. As for the emotions aroused by the play, surely they include both pity and *admiration* as well, perhaps, as fear. Corneille was attracted to epic actions and heroes as early as the *Cid* and in his next play after *Polyeucte,* that is, in *La Mort de Pompée,* he would make open use of an epic source: the *Pharsalia* of Lucan. In *Polyeucte* he conceals the link to Vergil's poem that we have examined in some detail; but he makes no attempt to hide the fact that his hero—a Christian and a martyr—is not a flawed hero.

This represents an essential point of disagreement between Corneille and Tasso. It does not rule out the influence of Tasso on *Polyeucte,* however; on the contrary, it seems in a way only to confirm it. For if Corneille himself is to join the company of the world's greatest poets, he must, even as Tasso himself did, reexamine the poetic heritage in whose wake he is traveling, keep what is true and valid, revise what is not, and in general renew rather than repeat the past. By giving his heroes a new, higher, Christian decorum, he rectifies the *Aeneid.* Since he shares with Tasso the same true religious faith that enlivens both the *Gerusalemme* and *Polyeucte,* he cannot aspire to introduce ethical or religious corrections to Tasso. He can, however, challenge the Italian poet's claim that epic and tragic poetry represent radically distinct genres that ought never to be mixed. I am not suggesting that Corneille would not have created an idealized, epic type hero if he had not read the *Discorsi.* As we have seen, his interest in ethical rectification goes back as far as *L'Illusion comique,* not to mention the *Cid* itself. I mean only to indicate that if Corneille was, in fact, intent on emulating Tasso, he need not have been upset by the idea of differing from Tasso. On the contrary, Tasso's idea of the *succession* of great poets implies a constant dialectic, so that by presuming to annex to tragedy certain sublime features that his predecessor had reserved for the epic, Corneille was really proving how well he had assimilated the main lesson of the *Discorsi.*[6]

We began in the previous chapter with a reading of *Polyeucte* based on book 4 of the *Aeneid* and end here with an examination of the play's relationship to the *Discorsi* of Tasso. There is, in this ordering, something like a fiction, something arbitrary in any event. For there is no way to tell whether Corneille actually began with the idea of rectifying the *Aeneid* and from there went on to the idea of recasting book 4 in terms of the life of a Christian saint. He might almost as well have proceeded contrariwise, and in all probability worked from both directions at the same time or in alternation, always adjusting the one perspective to the other. Act 4 of *Polyeucte* has two moments of sublimity: one, when Polyeucte weeps as he listens to Pauline's sad complaints; the other, a few moments later, when Pauline rejects all prospect of marriage to Sévère and instead enlists his aid in saving Polyeucte. The poetic processes by which the playwright created these and other great scenes in the play must lie forever beyond the ken of criticism to understand in all their complexity. Suffice it to say that the *Aeneid,* the *Discorsi,* the *Cid,* and the *Sentiments* appear to be useful texts for illuminating some of the central meanings of *Polyeucte.* Great poets do more than copy old poems or repeat their own earlier successes. They change what they touch, take things somehow always one step further than those who preceded them, become part of the living poetic (and therefore textual) tradition by renewing it. In *Polyeucte* Corneille makes what seems a conscious bid for greatness, and he calculates carefully his relationships to Vergil, to Tasso, and to the issues raised by the Quarrel at the same time that he takes the risk of striking out boldly on his own. In a more profound sense than Chapelain had meant, Corneille elected to treat his career as a magnificent heroic adventure; and *Polyeucte* can perhaps best be looked on as the poet's ultimate quest—and at the same time his greatest prize.

CHAPTER IV
The Roman Trilogy: Dante and Tasso

IN THE BID HE MADE FOR HIGH POETIC GREATNESS AFTER the Quarrel, Corneille turned to Vergil and Tasso, considered by most contemporary theorists, including Chapelain, as the very greatest of the great poets the world had ever produced. That both were epic poets would seem to indicate that, in the debate over the relative merits of epic poetry and tragedy, the generation of the *Cid* had opted for the epic (Bray, pp. 336–37). Corneille, who had begun his career as a dramatist, never showed signs of wanting to try his hand at the other, perhaps greater, genre. In the preceding chapter, however, we saw him eager to claim for the theater the perfect hero that Tasso had said belonged solely to epic poetry. The present chapter will propose another way in which Corneille tried to reap the advantages of the epic genre for his own.

Tasso takes up the debate over the relative merits of the two genres in the closing paragraphs of the *Discorsi*, summarizing the argument of Plato, the counterargument of Aristotle, and several lesser, later additions. Somewhat hesitantly, he ends up breaking with Aristotle in order to come down, as any reader of the *Discorsi* must guess he would have to, on the side of epic poetry. Epic poetry, he says, achieves its didactic ends more directly, therefore better, than tragedy. Of the pleasure created by the two genres, that of tragedy is more concentrated, that of epic poetry more dispersed; but the greater scope of epic poetry necessarily ensures for it a measure of preeminence: "è maggior virtù quella d'un corpo grande; così anco è maggiore il piacere dell'epopeia" (p. 258). This pleasure is, furthermore, not adulterated with tears and bitterness, as in tragedy; and though tragedy is simpler and more unified than epic poetry, it too possesses some degree of complexity and doubleness. And wherever the complex and the double exist, the most perfect structures are those that embrace and harmonize the greatest variety of different elements and qualities: "fra i corpi composti, quelli sono perfetti i quali sono misti e temperati di tutti gli elementi e di tutte le qualità, così aviene peraventura, tra le favole, che le più composte siano le migliori" (p. 259). Bigger is better not only at the end of the *Discorsi*, but pretty much throughout. Tasso opens book 2 with a reflection on the infinitude of possible poetic subjects and implies very clearly that it is the epic poet who can best exploit this great treasure house of subject matter:

> . . . Percioché Dante, innalzandosi dal centro, ascende sovra tutte le stelle fisse e sovra tutti i giri celesti; e Vergilio e Omero ci descrissero non solamente le cose che sono sotto la terra, ma quelle ancora che a pena con l'intelletto possiamo considerare; ma le ricoprirono con un gentilissimo velo d'allegoria. È dunque grandissima la varietà delle cose trattate da loro. . . . (p. 79)

If Corneille, as I am assuming, set out to compete with Vergil and Tasso, he could scarcely hope to do so with a single play, however great. He would need an *oeuvre* of a scope and a complexity comparable somehow to what characterizes the *Aeneid* and the *Gerusalemme*. A group of plays might serve the purpose, especially if they were interrelated in such a way as to constitute, to some extent, a single whole. The aim of what follows is to argue that *Horace, Cinna*, and *Polyeucte*, though they can obviously stand alone as viable works of art, were probably conceived as a trilogy, the better to make the case for their author as a world-class poet.

Three main themes bind the plays together as a group: Roman history, the idea of Providence, and heroic decorum. "Corneille se met à explorer systématiquement l'histoire de Rome," Maurens says. "Il peint ses débuts dans *Horace*, son apogée dans *Cinna*, et dans *Polyeucte* le conflit de l'empire avec la future civilisation chrétienne" (p. 252). (The critic adds, "On doute qu'il ait çoncu, dès 1639, cet ambitieux projet; et des raisons plus immédiates ont été à l'origine de son choix." But what more immediate reason could one ask for than the desire, with a really ambitious project like a trilogy, to silence once and for all the critics of the *Cid*?) The plays are linked, too, by the systematic way in which the heroes' actions are shown to carry more than their own ontological weight. Horace does not choose to fight; he is chosen. Auguste, rather than electing to launch a new policy of clemency, reacts to a vague discontent within himself and to the pressure of an unexpected situation from without; and at the height of his indecision, he commends himself to heaven: "Le ciel m'inspirera ce qu'ici je dois faire" (l. 1258). Polyeucte, for his part, seeks baptism only because, beforehand, he has felt descend upon him the grace of God. At the denouement of these same plays, providential support manifests itself again, this time to guarantee the authenticity of the heroes' claims and the high significance of their accomplishments. Tulle, in his self-proclaimed capacity as demigod, declares Horace a hero, in spite of the murder of Camille; Livie, who is inspired to prophecy, foresees the coming, under Auguste, of the Pax Romana; and the conversions of Pauline and Félix testify to the truth of the Christian faith for which Polyeucte was eager to die. All three plays deal, in short, with heroes who have a mission to perform and with missions that somehow transcend the individual heroes themselves.

The third system that links these plays depicts the heroes as embodying progressively higher forms of virtue, from the valor of Horace to the clemency of Auguste to the crowning glory of Christian charity in Polyeucte. The history of Rome and the heroes' moral ascent culminate simultaneously in the true religion of *Polyeucte*.

Now, these themes recur in many later plays of Corneille, but for the moment that is beside the point. What counts is how, and to what extent, they bind *Horace, Cinna,* and *Polyeucte* into some sort of unified whole. Nor is there only one vantage point from which to view this binding. Germain Poirier has proposed, as I do, that we read the plays as a trilogy, in a book that studies Corneille in the great tradition of philosophical moralists extending from Aristotle and Plato through Cicero to several of the Church Fathers (*Corneille et la vertu de prudence*). I want to continue to focus squarely on Corneille's perception of poetics and, more particularly, on his ambitious plan to emulate Tasso. To that end I shall reserve for later, separate consideration the matter of the plays' heroic ethos and shall begin by treating the first two themes together.

Critics have commented on the importance of Rome in Corneille's theater from the outset, and in our day three scholars in particular, Maurens, Stegmann, and Sweetser, have given serious attention to the role of Providence in Cornelian heroic dramaturgy. Except for M. Poirier, however, no one seems to have remarked on how these themes interact in *Horace, Cinna*, and *Polyeucte* to constitute a well-articulated view of Roman history as itself providentially inspired. Keeping to our vantage point of poetics, we can best understand what Corneille is doing if we compare his view of Roman history with what is found, first, in the *Aeneid* and, then, in two works of Dante, the *Convivio* and especially the *De Monarchia*.

C. S. Lewis makes the point that "all Roman epic before Vergil was probably metrical chronicle; and the subject was always the same—the coming-to-be of Rome." He goes on:

> What Vergil essentially did was to give this perennial theme a new unity by his symbolical structure. The *Aeneid* puts forward, though in mythical form, what is precisely a reading of history, an attempt to show what the *fata Jovis* were labouring to bring about. Everything is related not to Aeneas as an individual hero but to Aeneas as the Rome-bearer. This, and almost only this, gives significance to his escape from Troy, his *amour* with Dido, his descent into Hades, and his defeat of Turnus. *Tantae molis erat*, all history is for Vergil an immense parturition. (pp. 228–29)

One may specify even further the historical symbolism of the *Aeneid*. Dido and Turnus obviously represent obstacles to the hero's mission of founding Rome. One critic has gone so far as to say that in these two characters Vergil is depicting the "absorbing passion" on the one hand and the "high confidence" on the other that had to be sacrificed in order to have the empire of Augustus.[1] Anchises' revelations during the hero's descent into

Hades, like Venus's prophecy in book 1 and the allegory of Aeneas's shield in book 8, serves to extend to the whole of Rome's history lessons seen in the story of its founding father. And the *fata Jovis*, of course, operate throughout the poem to remind the reader that Roman history is in essence the story of the Roman people's divine mission.[2]

Corneille, by other means, achieves much the same effect as Vergil. Instead of using a single hero to embody the essential truth of Roman greatness, he chooses three, who together allow him to sum up the whole of Roman history. Each can be said, like Aeneas, to function as a "Rome-bearer." For just as Horace acts symbolically to give birth to primitive Rome—the Rome that first achieves hegemony over other city-states—so Auguste ushers in the new era of Roman empire and Polyeucte, the Christian dispensation that will bring the destiny of Rome to its ultimate perfection. Corneille endows his principal heroes with a deep respect for Roman traditions, coupled with an instinctive understanding of the need, also, for change and renewal, even at the expense of occasional violence. (Parturition, Corneille's theme as well as Vergil's, must always imply some degree of violence.)

In *Horace, Cinna,* and *Polyeucte,* Corneille does not yet have his heroes provide a running commentary on their own actions, as he will, for example, in *Rodogune.* Here his heroes act, and their actions make sense; but it is left to the spectator to decide exactly how. The playwright does, however, include several short passages evoking, after the fashion of the various symbolic foreshadowings of the *Aeneid,* the whole history of the Roman people, against which he wants us to view the story of the individual heroes. In the first scene of *Horace,* Sabine, an Alban by birth, reminds the audience of the greatness that lies ahead for Rome, whose dominion is destined to spread throughout the world, from the Pyrenees to the Orient, from the Rhine to the pillars of Hercules—after it subdues its competitors for power on the Italian peninsula (ll. 39–52). Livie's prophecy at the close of *Cinna* serves a similar purpose, foretelling the ultimate consolidation of world power under the peaceful reign of the emperor (ll. 1765–74). Polyeucte, for his part, though an Armenian and a Christian, has the greatest admiration for Rome and its traditions:

> Des aïeux de Décie [l'empereur] on vante la mémoire;
> Et ce nom, précieux encore à vos Romains,
> Au bout de six cents ans lui met l'empire aux mains.
> (4. 3. 1208–10)

His highest allegiance, however, belongs not to Rome but to God:

> Je dois ma vie au peuple, au prince, à sa couronne;
> Mais je la dois bien plus au Dieu qui me la donne:
> Si mourir pour son prince est un illustre sort,
> Quand on meurt pour son Dieu, quelle sera la mort!
> (4. 3. 1211–14)

Polyeucte, "bearer" of the last, Christian Rome—a Rome open to all who will accept its faith—comments only on the Rome of Augustus. It is Sévère who is charged at the very end of the play with foreshadowing the eventual Christianization of the empire:

> Je les aimai toujours [les chrétiens], quoi qu'on m'en ait pu
>   dire:
> Je n'en vois point mourir que ce coeur n'en soupire;
> Et peut-être qu'un jour je les connoîtrai mieux.
> J'approuve cependant que chacun ait ses Dieux,
> Qu'il les serve à sa mode, et sans peur de la peine.
> (5. 6. 1795–99)

Significantly, he leaves Félix, now converted, in charge of the state of Armenia:

> Servez bien votre Dieu, servez notre monarque.
> Je perdrai mon crédit envers Sa Majesté,
> Ou bien il quittera cette sévérité:
> Par cette injuste haine il se fait trop d'outrage.
> (5. 6. 1804–7)

Corneille takes Roman history beyond what Vergil saw as its divine culmination in the empire of Augustus, but for the moment the important thing is that the playwright, much like the epic poet before him, through the exploits of individual heroes is recounting in symbolic terms the divine story of Roman greatness. Corneille's *differences* from Vergil can perhaps best be approached through Dante, whose concept of Roman history, though Christian, owes a very great deal nevertheless to Vergil. Indeed, one critic has spoken of "l'appassionata interpretazione che il poeta fiorentino ha tracciato della storia romana, ispirandosi al poema virgiliano, citato da Dante colla stessa commossa riverenza con la quale e citata la Bibbia."[3] The Romans, like the Jews, are a chosen race for Dante; Providence presides over the history of both. The founding of the line of David coincides with the establishment of Rome by Aeneas (*Convivio* 4. 5); and the two histories converge at the moment of the birth of Christ, David's descendant, king of the Jews, Messiah, but also, as a man, subject to the temporal power of Rome, with his name inscribed on the official census rosters of the empire. In *De Monarchia* Dante is intent on proving the divine nature of the Roman Empire because he wants to see it revived in his own day, in tandem with the papacy as the ideal form of world government: "The Roman Empire was helped to its fulfillment by divine intervention and aid; therefore, it was willed by God and consequently existed and still exists by right" (2. 4). What Vergil and Roman historians had attributed to *fata Jovis*, Dante explicitly recuperates for Christian Providence preparing the way for the Coming of Christ. Such "miracles" as the hailstorm that kept Hannibal from destroying Rome or the cry of the goose that alerted the Capitoline guards to the approach of the Gauls become interventions of the Christian God: "It was fitting that He who foresees everything beautifully ordered in a single frame should work in this manner; that He, become visible in miracle, should make the invisible manifest, and being Himself invisible, should show Himself through these visible events" (2. 4). The divine power behind the action of *Horace* and *Cinna*—the power that inspires the choice of the combatants and that prompts Tulle to overlook Horace's crime; the power that impels Auguste to question the basis of his own authority and that later sends a vision of the future to Livie—this power has no explicitly defined source. It is attributed, that is, neither to Jove nor to God, but evasively and no doubt deliberately to the generic "Dieux" or "ciel." This very vagueness, however, facilitates the linking of *Horace* and *Cinna* to *Polyeucte* and the retroactive incorporation of the pagan into the Christian. It could not become apparent until *Polyeucte*, but *Horace* and *Cinna* may themselves also be seen as Christian plays. The Christian providential history of Rome, at least as Dante sees it, is ultimately seamless and all-inclusive.

Admittedly, Corneille does not say, as Dante does, that this is the interpretation he intends. The aim of dramatic poetry being to move rather than to inform and persuade, there is no reason why Corneille should explicate his allegory (if indeed allegory is the term for it). Nothing in the text of *Horace, Cinna,* and *Polyeucte* either proves outright, or is in contradiction with, the hypothesis, however; and the concordance of views seems to me very close—too close to be accidental. And there is also one more point to take into account: the likelihood that Dante gave Corneille the idea for the subjects of *Horace* and *Cinna,* the two pre-Christian plays in his trilogy.

The history of Rome, for Dante, is the story of its gradual acquisition of power until it becomes the sole power in the whole world. God, who oversees this expansion, gives periodic signs to man that guarantee and justify the Roman state (2. 1–12). The greatest of these signs is the birth of Christ, which bestows upon the empire of Augustus a unique importance in the total scheme of things (2. 11–12). A Christian view of the history of Rome could never exclude Augustus, and Corneille does not. What serves to justify Roman expansion in its earlier phases is something else: primarily, the adherence to prescribed rules of combat. These rules, according to Dante, are those that traditionally governed the *duellum* (2. 9–10). That is, each side, in order to avoid unnecessary bloodshed, would designate champions to represent them; and these combatants, fighting without enmity, would be the instruments by which Providence would show which side was destined to triumph. Dante sees Roman history as a succession of such encounters, of increasingly large numbers of champions, all of them faithful to the spirit of the first *duellum.* He lists six such encounters in particular: two pitting the Roman people, on a world scale, against the Greeks and the Carthaginians; two opposing the Romans, in an earlier period, to the neighboring tribes of the Sabines and the Samnites; and two very early, small-scale combats—the first between Aeneas and Turnus, the second between the Horatii and the Curiatii (2.10).[4]

In *Polyeucte,* as we have seen, Corneille undertook to rectify book 4 of the *Aeneid.* The evidence we have examined so far in the present chapter points to a broader hypothesis: that the playwright was aiming, in the group of three plays, at something like rectification of the whole of the *Aeneid.* Dante, who had already taken Vergil's central idea of Roman history and transformed it into a profoundly Christian story, could have served the playwright as a guide. Tasso, in the *Discorsi,* had recommended that the modern poet choose a subject from the history of the Middle Ages: Charlemagne or Arthur, rather than Theseus or Jason. Corneille's choice, instead, of the whole of Roman history, though it seems to flout this advice, in fact is not really at odds with it at all. For what Tasso wanted was for the poet to treat a Christian theme and one that, for practical purposes, would be neither too close nor too far away from the audience. *Horace, Cinna,* and *Polyeucte,* I have argued, do have a Christian subject, though one that cannot be seen in the first two plays except retroactively, from the vantage point of *Polyeucte.* As for the question of remoteness, Corneille's public felt more affinity with Rome than with the Middle Ages. And, in any event, Corneille really uses Roman history poetically, as a metaphor to stand for the entirety of man's historical experience.

There remains now to be considered the third important element linking the three plays, namely, heroic decorum.[5] This decorum very obviously evolves from play to play. Corneille assumes a hierarchy of virtues and, within this hierarchy, shows a gradual ascent to perfection. Horace has the virtues of a warrior—valor, fortitude, cunning; Auguste, the virtues of a man of peace—clemency, justice, magnanimity. The ones are necessary for the acquisition of power, the others for its wise administration. Horace, for all his virtue, commits, within the play, a terrible crime that places in jeopardy his very reputation as a hero. Auguste also carries with him a burden of criminality, but it dates from a now-distant past and functions in the play only as a bad memory. Polyeucte, on the other hand, is entirely without crime or flaw; and he embodies what for a Christian may be the highest of all virtues: faith in God and love of man. (He dies in order to testify so that others may be saved after him.)

This hierarchical ordering of heroic decorum has no equivalent in either the *Aeneid* or *De Monarchia.* Vergil regards the empire as the glorious culmination of all the heroic struggles of the Roman people since Aeneas; but while the size and constitution of the state undergo change over the centuries, the heroic nature of the Roman character remains a constant, equally fulfilled in Aeneas and Augustus. Similarly, for Dante, there appears to be no ethical difference between early heroes like Aeneas or the Horatii and later ones like Fabricius or Scipio: all exemplify the very best in Rome. Of course, Dante does treat the theme of spiritual ascent, in fact ascent in three stages, in the *Divina commedia*; and it is not impossible to find rough equivalents of Inferno, Purgatory, and Paradise in Corneille's three plays. Horace, it will be recalled, is condemned to *live*—and to consider, with a tormenting sense of deprivation, a moment of supreme fulfillment that will lie forever in the past. Auguste, along with all the other characters in *Cinna*, experiences meanwhile something very much like purgation and, at the denouement, emerges cleansed, absolved, and renewed; and Polyeucte, the last manifestation of the playwright's composite Roman hero, through martyrdom, is transported into Heaven.

The moral hierarchy in Corneille's trilogy is suggestive most of all, however, of the evolutionary changes in heroic decorum that Tasso saw in the *Discorsi*. Horace, to be sure, is not a copy of Achilles. Corneille specifically denies to his first Roman hero the terrible wrath that characterizes Homer's protagonist. As a pre-Christian hero and participant in the providentially inspired history of Rome, Horace must and does adhere completely to the spirit of the *duellum*, which is never fought in hatred. But he is above all else a warrior, like Achilles; and his motives are often misunderstood. Those around him accuse him of being inhuman or barbarous; Sabine credits his slaying of Camille to an outburst of anger: "A quoi s'arrête ici ton illustre colère" (l. 1335). Similarly Auguste and Polyeucte are not modeled in any direct way on Aeneas or, for example, Godefroy de Bouillon. Auguste ends up with many of the same virtues that Tasso attributed to the hero of the *Aeneid*, but Aeneas is a paragon of heroic qualities from the outset. And Polyeucte, no less than Auguste, has none of the military encounters that loom so important in the poems of Vergil and Tasso. One-to-one comparisons of the heroes, though occasionally interesting, do not lead far and are not very important. What is important, I think, is the similarity of the interrelationships of the two triads of heroes. Horace, Auguste, and Polyeucte relate to one another just as Achilles, Aeneas, and the modern Christian hero do, as heroes whose virtues embody a progressively higher, more authentic vision of man in his relation to the world and to God. I have said before that Corneille may have conceived the trilogy as a means of positing an *oeuvre* of epic-like scope. That in itself would have been a very ambitious project for so young a poet. If one accepts in addition that the trilogy he wrote aspires in effect to recapitulate the whole history of heroic poetry—from the *Iliad* to the *Aeneid* to the *Gerusalemme*—then his achievement becomes even more astounding.

It is not, I think, going too far to claim this much for Corneille.[6] The idea of summarizing all previous heroic poetry in a single new poem would seem to go hand in hand with the idea of compressing all history, pagan and Christian alike, into one history, the history of the Roman people. Both attest to the playwright's vigorous universalizing imagination. No less remarkable than this power to integrate material, however, is the poet's capacity also to renew and to innovate. For he assimilates totally whatever he borrows, and he borrows with great audacity across generic lines, thereby extending the range not only of tragedy but of epic poetry too.

Chapelain had labored to see that something good should come out of the acrimonious dispute over the *Cid*. To Corneille he had preached the benefits that might accrue from adverse (but not hostile) criticism: "Le blasme . . . dessille les yeux de l'homme que l'amour propre luy avoit fermés, et luy faisant voir combien il est esloigné du bout de la carriere, l'excite à redoubler ses efforts pour y parvenir" (Gasté, p. 356). He granted strengths to the *Cid*, offered suggestions as to how its deficiencies might be overcome, and recommended to the beleaguered but talented young poet the example of Tasso to follow. He even indicated at one point that Corneille ought to look upon his career as an adventure. What he never envisioned, because his own imagination and daring could scarcely take him half the distance, was a heroic undertaking of the magnitude and complexity of *Horace, Cinna*, and *Polyeucte*. Corneille's gamble was a heroic gamble, entailing the greatest risks but promising also the highest rewards. That his contemporaries thought he had won is proved by the existence of the decorated cabinet made for Mazarin, with its portraits of the world's four greatest poets: Homer, Vergil, Tasso, and Corneille.

CHAPTER V
La Mort de Pompée:
Lucan and Tasso

AFTER THE FAILURE OF *PERTHARITE* IN 1652 AND A SUBSE-
quent seven-year retirement, Corneille returned to the theater
triumphantly in 1659 with *Oedipe*. When he published the play
the following year, he prefaced it with a little poem that purports
to explain the genesis of the work. Foucquet, it would appear,
had urged Corneille to resume his interrupted career; and the
playwright, accepting the challenge, had replied in verse. In the
poem he begins by thanking Foucquet for his confidence and
reassures him that, because of him, the poetic fire that once produced heroes like Rodrigue, Horace, Pompée, and Cinna has
been rekindled. All the poet needs now is a proper subject, and
he asks that his new patron agree to choose the hero for his next
play:

> Choisis-moi seulement quelque nom dans l'histoire
> Pour qui tu veuilles place au temple de la Gloire,
> Quelque nom favori qu'il te plaise arracher
> A la nuit de la tombe, aux cendres du bûcher.
> Soit qu'il faille ternir ceux d'Enée et d'Achille
> Par un noble attentat sur Homère et Virgile,
> Soit qu'il faille obscurcir par un dernier effort
> Ceux que j'ai sur la scène affranchis de la mort:
> Tu me verras le même, et je te ferai dire,
> Si jamais pleinement ta grande âme m'inspire,
> Que dix lustres et plus n'ont pas tout emporté
> Cet assemblage heureux de force et de clarté,
> Ces prestiges secrets de l'aimable imposture
> Qu'à l'envi m'ont prêtée et l'art et la nature.
> (*Oeuvres*, 6: 122–23, ll. 37–50)

These few lines provide an invaluable insight into their author's aesthetic psychology, and a confirmation of things already seen. They tell us, for one thing, that Corneille is alternately proud (of his ability to make the past relive on the stage) and humble (inasmuch as he depends on a patron for inspiration). They indicate, moreover, that the poet does not think of inventing characters or situations, but only of re-creating heroes borrowed from the pages of history or earlier literature. Finally, they suggest that the goal of re-creation is somehow to improve on the past. Corneille is ready, if Foucquet is willing, to make a "noble assault" on Homer and Vergil and dim the glory that surrounds Achilles and Aeneas—or to give new luster to one of his own earlier creations. As we have seen in the preceding chapters, Corneille did not wait for Foucquet to set him to the task of trying to outdo Homer and Vergil; he had already organized a noble assault on their poetic redoubts and on Tasso's, too, in the Roman trilogy. Nor did the playwright have to be told to borrow from himself; as we also know, he revised the Jason of *Médée* to produce the hero of the little tragedy in *L'Illusion comique.* The options offered to Foucquet are the same as those that Corneille had been entertaining for himself all along.

Corneille's attitude here implies a constant vying with others and with oneself. The poet must not just do something different—that in itself would be difficult enough and, after a while, tiring—he must strive always to surpass or outshine the past, including his own. This obsession with pushing poetic achievement to ever-new heights produced in Corneille his original ambition to emulate Homer, Vergil, and Tasso and led to the creation of the group of plays by which, I have suggested, he hoped to prove himself their successor and their peer. It brought with it, however, a serious problem, to which there was really no solution. What nobler assault was there left to attempt once the assault of these giants of poetic history had been made? Corneille had reached so far so fast after the Quarrel that in a sense he had exhausted all further possibilities for still greater achievement in the future. After the tremendous effort of the trilogy, he must have felt left over, much like Horace in the aftermath of his supreme moment of glory on the battlefield against Alba. Or like Moses, once he had come down from the mountaintop. Some critics have denied that there is a falling off of power in Corneille's theater after *Polyeucte.* They are mistaken, I think. The next three plays show the playwright charting an essentially rudderless course. By his own admission he was writing not out of any strong inner drive but rather in response to various particular observations or proposals. He wrote *La Mort de Pompée,* he said, "pour satisfaire à ceux qui ne trouvoient pas les vers de *Polyeucte* si puissants que ceux de *Cinna*" (Epître for *Le Menteur*); *Le Menteur,* "pour contenter les souhaits de beaucoup d'autres qui ont demandé quelque chose de plus enjoué qui ne servît qu'à les divertir" (ibid.); and *La Suite du Menteur,* obviously, in order to exploit the success of *Le Menteur.* With *Rodogune* he was to launch a new phase of his career, but neither *Rodogune* nor *Nicomède* nor *Sertorius* nor any other later work was ever able to eclipse the achievement of *Horace, Cinna,* and *Polyeucte* or of *Le Cid.* One must face, as Corneille did, the truth of a relative decline in his theater after the triumph of the trilogy.

In his critical writing, Corneille often provides fascinating details on how he went about creating this or that desired dramatic effect. Like a magician explaining the tricks of the trade, he takes the reader into his confidence, shows what he started with, what adjustments he introduced, and finally the extent to which the ensuing theatrical spell succeeded. The persona of the kindly artificer who is willing to tell all is engaging, but it is sometimes as much of an artifice as the illusion that is supposedly being explained. A case in point is *Polyeucte,* in connection with which the playwright breathes not a word about its relation to the *Aeneid.* Another instance is *La Mort de Pompée,* his next play. In several early editions, Corneille not only identifies his ancient source—Lucan's epic poem, the *Pharsalia*—but specifies a large number of verses that he either translated or closely imitated from the Latin poet. And he hints that the principal artistic problem he had confronted in working with the *Pharsalia* lay in the need to compress the epic's sprawling subject: the play, he said in the Au Lecteur, was an "effort pour réduire en poème dramatique ce que [Lucain] a traité en épique." In fact he incurred another debt in writing the play, a debt that goes unmentioned. For if the major incidents and characters derive from Lucan—ultimately from Roman history, since the *Pharsalia* does not greatly embellish the historical data—the perspective in which he places them comes from the modern Christian epic, about which he says nothing. And what is most problematic about the play is certainly the resulting unstable mixture of contradictory elements. Critics, stymied by the work, have disagreed about such fundamental points as whether César's *générosité* is authentic or feigned or whether the denouement is didactic, on the one hand, or ambiguous, on the other.[1] The playwright's remarks have not caused this confusion, but neither have they really clarified the play or prevented misconstruction. If we look at *Pompée* in the context of the author's emulation of Tasso, perhaps it will make more sense.

The message of the *Pharsalia* is a clear one, repeated over and over in every aspect of the poem, including its other title *De Bello Civili.* Civil war is an unnatural thing, a horrible thing. It represents a primal disregard for the sacredness of the most basic boundaries, those that separate brothers from one another only to ensure the individual freedom of all. When César crosses the Rubicon, he violates not only a geographical but also a political and a psychological barrier, igniting a war of brother against brother aimed at overthrowing the republic and putting in its place an imperial form of government with César at the helm. Incident after incident, image after image, points to the universality of the poet's condemnation, which extends even to those, like Pompée, who fight for the right cause. Civil war, the poet cries out, is an abomination, and it looses on the world a horde of other, like disorders. Pompée's murder at the hands of treacherous Egyptians has a special narrative significance: it marks the disappearance from the story of one of the two principal antagonists. But, ideologically, it is in no way a "privileged" crime; it is only another in a seemingly endless chain of disasters, traceable ultimately to the original outbreak of civil war in Rome.

This message is not the message—or at least not the main message—of Corneille's play. The theme of *Pompée* is quite different: the assertion of Roman greatness and unity in the face of the attack by the Egyptians. The earlier conflict, especially at Pharsalus, is not forgotten, and there are plans to continue the struggle elsewhere at a later date. But most important within the play itself are César's magnanimous gestures toward Cornélie— he gives orders for her to be treated like a head of state and

undertakes to punish her dead husband's murderers—and Cornélie's equally noble action in warning César of an Egyptian plot
against his life. Much of *Pompée* is in fact a kind of anti-*Pharsalia.*
The assertion of Roman greatness as opposed to Egyptian criminality is the insertion of Roman greatness into Lucan's story of
Rome's decline into civil war. This reversal of thematic scheme is
of infinitely greater importance than the narrowing of epic
scope, and the change has nothing to do directly with passing
from one poetic genre to another.

Pompée eschews the dramaturgy of *Horace, Cinna,* and
Polyeucte, in which the action moved forward to a denouement
with reconciliation (Sweetser, *Dramaturgie,* p. 127). It sets up a
series of dichotomies of such rigidity as to preclude all possibility of a complete solution. The five principal characters are all
illustrious historical figures. They are differentiated sharply,
however, by national origin and ethical persuasion. They are
either Roman or Egyptian, noble- or mean-spirited. Rome is the
seat of disinterested virtue; Egypt, the center of villainous criminality. There are two crossover characters: a turncoat Roman,
who is one of Ptolomée's evil advisers; and Cléopâtre, who
manifests a *générosité* in every way worthy of Rome. The dichotomies persist, however, and never cease to govern the structure of the dramatic conflict.[2]

Neither Lucan nor the earlier practice of Corneille himself
can account for this dichotomous view of the world in *Pompée.*
The view conforms nearly perfectly, however, to the requirements set forth in the *Discorsi* for the plot structure of the ideal
epic poem. We have already seen that Tasso advises the modern,
Christian poet to choose a Christian hero, Charlemagne or Arthur, instead of Theseus or Jason, to ensure that the hero will
more naturally embody all the perfections expected of him. Opposite this hero, representing "il sommo de le virtù," Tasso sets
an antihero who embodies, for his part, "l'eccellenza del vizio";
and the plot describes the clear-cut struggle that grows up between them (pp. 98, 103). The ideal epic story involves the contest of Christians against infidels: "a i nostri tempi le vittorie de'
fideli contro gli infideli porgeranno gratissimo e nobilissimo ar-
gumento di poetare" (p. 98). It follows from Tasso's adoption of
a system of two extreme "conditions" that, much more insistently than Aristotle, he will repeat that the denouement must

involve a double reversal, whereby the "fideli" go from bad fortune to good and the "infideli," conversely, from good fortune to bad. The insertion that Corneille makes into the Lucan story entails the assertion of a system of ethics and aesthetics that is clearly Tassoan. Rome and Egypt stand opposed to each other like Christendom and the Moslem world in the *Discorsi* (or in the *Gerusalemme liberata*). Corneille, we shall see in detail later, has ennobled the Roman figures that history and Lucan passed on to him. The Romans now embody—or are on their way to embodying—the highest of virtues, whereas the Egyptians—Ptolomée and his advisers—become the incarnation of vice. Each group meets, or tends to meet, the end it deserves. The king and his advisers die violently, whereas the Romans not only survive but survive by defending one another, and in so doing they reaffirm the heroic greatness that their internal dissension has called into question.

The denouement of Corneille's inserted story does not coincide with the denouement of the play, however; the play includes not only the inserted material but the original story as well. The critics' contradictory readings of the denouement probably derive in large part from a failure to see that the play gives us two plays—and thus two denouements—in one. The Tassoan play may be said to start with the deliberation scene, a favorite topos of the epic, and to end with the news of Ptolomée's drowning, whereas the Lucan play extends from the battle at Pharsalus to Cornélie's departure for Libya to resume the civil conflict. Some critics argue that the ending of *Pompée* is didactic; but only the inserted, Tassoan part, which celebrates the superiority of Roman virtues over Egyptian vices, is in fact didactic. Other critics have stressed those passages of the play that bring the action back to historical fact and to Lucan—back, in other words, to a continuation of hostilities within Rome. For them, the denouement is "ambiguous," although the ambiguity often goes unexplained.[3]

Actually, we should understand the insertion of one story into another not as an isolated event but rather as a continuing process. Corneille does not start with Lucan, then stop abruptly to pick up Tasso, only to turn back mechanically to Lucan. All through the play he is constantly manipulating the Lucan (historical) material, trying to make it fit the Tassoan mold. Thus the denouement presents only one of the problems of interpretation that occur throughout the play. Not a few interpreters have fallen victim to the temptation to assume a unity, or a kind of unity, that is not in the text and, in effect, resolve the existing ambiguities into either an optimistic, upbeat Tassoan reading or a more pessimistic, downbeat Lucan reading. We should bear in mind that both polarities exist in the play at almost every moment and that what we need is a sense of how the dramatic energy of the play flows between them.

The basic tension in the play is not resolved completely, nor could it have been. At several points—including, but not restricted to, the denouement—the historical facts simply cannot be adjusted or rectified to the Tassoan requirements. Corneille seems to have undertaken something that in some measure was doomed to failure. What remains to be seen, along with further details of how the play modulates between its two polarities, is whether Corneille intended *Pompée* to "fail."

For Voltaire as well as for a number of recent critics, *Pompée* has so little dramatic action that it verges on historical tableau.[4] I shall return to this question later; for now, this criticism of the play suggests that the best initial approach may well lie through the characters rather than through the plot. We have seen, in general, what the dramatic framework of *Pompée* is and how it implies the juxtaposing of Lucan and Tassoan elements. Let us look at how the play's five principal historical figures take their places within this overall scheme. These figures are Pompée (who appears only through *récits*), César, Cornélie, Cléopâtre, and Ptolomée. Of these Pompée and Ptolomée have undergone the least substantial change in passing from the *Pharsalia* into Corneille's play. Since Lucan admired Pompée and despised Ptolomée, they already tended to fit into the pattern of the all-virtuous versus the all-wicked. Nevertheless, Lucan's admiration for Magnus, as he invariably calls Pompée, is by no means absolute; and in the poet's mind, Pompée shares with César the heavy responsibility for plunging Rome into its sickening conflict. Corneille suppresses virtually all mention of weakness of will, error of judgment, or doubtful motive, and by thus eliminating the shadows in Lucan casts the martyred hero in an especially bright virtuous light. One would expect in Ptolomée a counterbalancing intensification of evil, but Corneille complicates the symmetry by depicting the young Egyptian king as more weak than wicked. It is Ptolomée's advisers, on whom he is overly dependent, who most fully personify "l'eccellenza del vizio." If Ptolomée had trusted to his own best instincts, Corneille suggests at several points, he could have avoided the ignominy to which he eventually falls. The conventions of the modern epic control Ptolomée, within the play, as an Egyptian; as a king, however, he reflects the prevailing ideology in France concerning providential support for the monarchy. Ptolomée's Egyptianness is what finally dominates, and it is fitting that he should join his evil advisers in death.[5]

The role of Cornélie has sometimes been looked on as a tedious exercise in rhetorical inflation. It was once a favorite of actresses, however, and on close examination proves considerably more complex than is generally thought. The role provides, for one thing, an excellent vantage point from which to watch the playwright rectifying Lucan (or history) to a Tassoan mold. Whereas history records that Cornélie arrived in Egypt with her husband, witnessed his murder from shipboard, then immediately set sail for Libya, hotly pursued by Ptolomée's emissaries, Corneille has the pursuing Egyptians catch her, bring her back to court, and hand her over to César on his arrival. César delays her further so that she can see that he has adequately punished her husband's murderers. In historical chronology this change has no great importance, since the delay lasts only a day. Within the play, however, which is limited to a single revolution of the sun, the change makes all the difference in the world. Through this alteration Corneille opens up in the Lucan story an interstice quite large enough for a whole other story to start to emerge, the story of Roman virtues reasserting themselves against the murky background of Egyptian intrigue; in short, the Tassoan epic story.

Within this overall scheme, Cornélie manifests three main aspects of character. Throughout the play she remains what she was in the *Pharsalia*, a pathetic emblem of the suffering brought on by civil strife. Devoted to Rome, she has seen it rent asunder by internal wars; devoted also to her husband, she has witnessed his dismemberment at the hands of the Egyptians. She is, then, first and last a widow; and at the beginning of act 5, Corneille, following Garnier, gives Cornélie a touching, ornate apostrophe (to her husband's remains) that everyone remembers.

This widow also exemplifies stoic fortitude. She does not collapse under the burden of her misfortune but rather steels herself to continue alone from where her husband has left off. A recent editor of *Pompée* has remarked on the absence of a historical basis for Cornélie's stoicism and has suggested that Corneille may want us to assume that she learned her stoicism, in some unspecified way, through Cato, with whom Pompée had been associated politically (Barnwell, pp. 62, 162 n. to line 476). The link need not be left so vaguely defined as this, however. In book 9 of the *Pharsalia*, Cato plays a crucial role as designated successor to the fallen Magnus. Up to this point Cato has refrained from taking sides; but, since no one else is able to assume the leadership left vacant by Pompée's death and since the Republican cause for which Pompée fought was after all the better of the two, Cato resolves to step into the breach himself. And in a moving speech in praise of the fallen leader and his cause, Cato offers himself as Pompée's heir and rallies the Pompeian forces to continue the fight. Corneille could not incorporate this action into the play directly without violating the unities; yet he had to establish that the war would be waged again after the Egyptian "interlude" came to a close. Corneille introduces this idea indirectly, through Cornélie. It is she who resolves not to accept the defeat at Pharsalus as definitive, she who proclaims the firm intention to fight again another day on another field of battle. And she inherits Cato's stoical character, together with his dramatic function.

If Cornélie is determined ultimately to get revenge against César, she is nevertheless willing, even eager, to suspend her efforts until the moment is more propitious. Cornélie is thus also *généreuse*. We see her *générosité* first in her acceptance of César's magnanimity: "O ciel, que de vertus vous me faites haïr!" (l. 1072). We see it again, more dramatically, when she refuses to acquiesce in an Egyptian plot against César's life and instead warns him of the danger. "O coeur vraiment romain," says César, "Et digne du héros qui vous donna la main" (ll. 1363–64). Cornélie will pursue his downfall, but only in the open and by honorable means, and she scorns the idea of owing anything to the Egyptians.

We learn after the fact (in act 5) that when Cornélie intervened earlier to save César, she did so despite her doubts about the genuineness of his magnanimity. Informed by Philippe of César's public concern for the physical remains of Pompée, part of which have just been recovered, Cornélie remarks that César's magnanimity toward her and toward his dead rival has cost him nothing and may indeed only cover his self-interest. His show of indignation against the Egyptians has strengthened his hold over Egypt and may have been calculated to that end. Cornélie cannot determine what César's real motives are. Nevertheless, she chooses to believe him:

> Tant d'intérêts [personnels] sont joints à ceux de mon époux,
> Que je ne devrois rien à ce qu'il fait pour nous,
> Si, comme par soi-même un grand coeur juge un autre,
> Je n'aimois mieux juger sa vertu par la nôtre,
> Et croire que nous seuls armons ce combattant [= César],
> Parce qu'au point qu'il est j'en voudrois faire autant.
>
> (5. 1. 1551–56)

Cornélie makes what amounts to a Pascalian wager. Her *générosité* takes her beyond stoical resolve to bear up courageously under the onslaughts of bad fortune; even when she cannot establish the facts with total clarity, she proves ready to commit herself fully. Her ethic is proud and aristocratic, and it acknowledges forthrightly the need to take risks. La Rochefoucauld, who was also well acquainted with bad fortune, knowing how bitter life's disillusionments could be, wrote, "Il est plus honteux de se défier de ses amis que d'en être trompé" (no. 84). César is not a friend, but he is a fellow Roman; and Cornélie "elects" to believe the best of him. The leap of faith marks what is most admirable in Cornélie; it also reveals what is most modern and most nearly Christian.

The role is thus a complex combination of virtues: wifely devotion and stoical fortitude (both of which derive from Lucan, though the stoicism comes through contamination of the role with that of Cato) and, finally, a *générosité* that far exceeds anything in the *Pharsalia*. The sum of all these virtues makes Cornélie a true "sommo de le virtù"; and, opposite her, the Egyptians with their deep-seated fears and their panicky recourse to treachery cannot help but appear to the audience as both grotesque and contemptible, "l'eccellenza del vizio."

Concerning César, it is important to note first of all that in the *Pharsalia* there is no doubt at all about his motivations. Thus, when the Egyptians show him the severed head of Pompée,

> Caesar did not turn away or reject the gift, but closely scruti-
> nized the well-known features which had shrunk since death,
> until he could be satisfied that they were indeed Pompey's.
> When no doubt remained and he thought it safe at last to play
> the loving father-in-law [Caesar's daughter had been Pom-
> pey's first wife], he forced out tears and groans—his readiest
> means of disguising too obvious a joy. (9. 1036–41)

In Corneille's play Achorée gives a different account of the same incident:

> . . . Par un mouvement commun à la nature,
> Quelque maligne joie en son coeur s'élevoit,
> Dont sa gloire indignée à peine le sauvoit.
> . . . .
> S'il aime sa grandeur, il hait la perfidie;
> Il se juge en autrui, se tâte, s'étudie,
> Consulte à sa raison sa joie et ses douleurs,
> Examine, choisit, laisse couler des pleurs;
> Et forçant sa vertu d'être encore la maîtresse,
> Se montre généreux par un trait de foiblesse.
>
> (3. 1. 774–86)

The distance between Lucan and Corneille is substantial. The César of *Pompée* is a man who struggles not to hide an igno-ble emotion but to overcome it. Granted that the paths of self-interest and of *générosité* coincide, Corneille has nevertheless replaced Lucan's clear-cut but negative motivation in the *Pharsa-lia* with at least the possibility of true nobility of character in *Pompée*.[6]

If César were characterized only by his (somewhat dubious) *générosité*, his would be a weak role indeed, totally subsidiary to that of Cornélie. But beyond all question of *générosité*, he exem-plifies two other distinct aspects of the heroic character, wrath and love. These, we know from chapter 3, above, represent for Tasso, respectively, the ancient and the modern heroic virtues par excellence; and Corneille has quite deliberately juxtaposed them in re-creating the figure of César. Ptolomée and Ptolomée's advisers look upon César as a constant embodiment of wrath and refer obsessively to his *colère* or his *courroux*. The king quakes in his presence and ends up begging Cléopâtre to intercede for the lives of the advisers. When the Egyptians decide to try to kill César, they know that success will depend on opposing his wrath with an even stronger Egyptian wrath. They disastrously miscalculate their resources, but they have a clear picture of the grounds on which they must engage the combat. Even the Roman they have martyred returns and confounds their puny efforts to emulate true courage, for the severed head they present to César is said still to bear an expression of anger, directed beyond his Egyptian assailants to the gods in heaven who permitted such treachery. Wrath thus functions in the play as a "Roman" virtue, seen in both Roman leaders but especially in the survivor and avenger, César.

The playwright's skills are tested more seriously when it comes to making César not only wrathful but also loving, especially with the new type of love that alone was deemed heroic. Vestiges of the historical, Lucan view of the liaison between César and Cléopâtre persist, particularly in the parting speech of Cornélie at the close of the play. Having once more assumed her role as avenger of Pompée, Cornélie rededicates herself to ensuring the eventual defeat of her great civil enemy, with or without the help of the gods. If all else should fail, she says, perhaps Cléopâtre with her entanglements may prove the instrument of his fall from power. The lovers take this prospect seriously after Cornélie exits, for César and Cléopâtre are much aware of Rome's opposition to their love. But Cornélie's desperate malediction notwithstanding, that love, as we see it throughout most of the rest of the play, is quite obviously Tassoan.[7] Cléopâtre, though in love with César, argues early in the play for granting asylum to his enemy Pompée. Because she owes a debt to Pompée for the help he gave her father, she cannot act otherwise and still merit esteem in her own and César's eyes. Her love for César, like his for her, is thus no base passion but a product of mutually recognized nobility of will, in seventeenth-century terms *amour-estime*. The lovers' one great scene together, delayed until act 4, is a celebration of their love as a source of strength for the hero, even in the military sphere. César proclaims that it is not ambition but the desire to merit Cléopâtre that ultimately motivates all he has done or plans to do on the battlefields of the world:

C'étoit pour acquérir un droit si précieux
Que combattoit partout mon bras ambitieux;
Et dans Pharsale même il a tiré l'épée
Plus pour le conserver que pour vaincre Pompée.

(4. 3. 1267–70)

Permettez cependant qu'à ces douces amorces
Je prenne un nouveau coeur et de nouvelles forces,
Pour faire dire encore aux peuples pleins d'effroi,
Que venir, voir et vaincre est même chose en moi.

(4. 3. 1333–36)

It is a misreading of these famous lines to say they are intended to "humanize" the hero by showing that he is subject to ordinary. human weaknesses.[8] They are in the play to do precisely the contrary, to render the hero even more heroic, as Tasso specifies: "Laonde azioni eroiche ci potranno parer, oltre l'altre, quelle che son fatte per amore" (p. 106). César's military conquests are indubitably illustrious by any reckoning, including Lucan's. What Corneille adds here is the attempt to elevate them still more by attributing them ultimately to love. The scene fails, in that it does not realize poetically its enunciated ideological convictions. The tone is wrong. As Voltaire suggests, César sounds too much like a gallant wandered in from some seventeenth-century novel.[9] There is too much, or the wrong kind of, wit. "Vous pouvez d'un coup d'oeil désarmer sa colère," Ptolomée says to his sister as César arrives; and the latter excuses his tardiness with a too playful reference to heroic anger: "Et ces soins importuns, qui m'arrachoient de vous,/Contre ma grandeur même allumoient mon courroux" (ll. 1247–48). No, there is no trifling with heroic love. For all his genius, Corneille is not proof against occasional lapses in taste and judgment. His failure here to find the right mode of poetic expression should not, however, obscure his goal, which is to show a virtuous, "Roman" César in whom an idealized love joins with wrath and magnanimity to form a new type of epic hero, at least in the Tassoan part of the play.

Cléopâtre, the last character to be considered, has little to do in the play except love César and be loved by him. She refuses to take part in her brother's plot against Pompée, but she is in no position to hinder it. She desires her rightful share of the royal power, resists Ptolomée's attempts to divest her of her sovereignty, and ends up as the sole occupant of the throne, but her success in resisting Ptolomée results more from Ptolomée's mistakes than from her own calculations. Her role could easily be dispensed with—except that she does add illustriousness to the play, and the Tassoan epic hero does require someone to love. There are two interesting aspects to her role, however: one is her *générosité*, which is much more important in the play than her ambition;[10] the other is the impediment to her marriage with César. Cléopâtre is *généreuse* because as a royal personage she was born with an innate *générosité*, to which, unlike Ptolomée, she has elected to remain true. In addition, Corneille amends history, giving both Cléopâtre and her brother an earlier sojourn in Rome, when their father sought the help of the Roman senate against his rebellious subjects. It was during this time that César first caught sight of Cléopâtre and fell in love with her. Cléopâtre herself had come back to Egypt with a confirmed sense of her own greatness and deep admiration for Rome. In the play her *générosité* makes her Roman in spirit if not in fact; indeed, César could not love her with an *amour-estime* if she lacked this *générosité*. An ancient Roman law, however, with which the lovers and Cornélie are all familiar, forbids marriage between a ruler of Rome and a foreign monarch.[11] So long as this law stands unchallenged, there can be little hope for the lovers' happiness, no matter how much they love and "deserve" each other.

Contrary to what history and Lucan recount, Corneille's lovers do not consider the possibility of an amorous liaison outside marriage. What César does propose is to try to change the law. Lucan sees César as totally lacking in respect for the traditions and institutions of Rome. Corneille presents the Roman leader in a different light. The play does not explore the political implications of the change in Rome from republic to empire, and César's desire to strike the marriage law from the books consequently seems natural. The impediment to marriage is judged within the play primarily from the point of view of the lovers themselves, with Cornélie alluding only at the very end to the possibility of Roman resistance to such a move. The love between César and Cléopâtre is the equivalent of the love that one finds between a Christian hero and a Saracen princess in modern epic poems like the *Gerusalemme liberata*—with the important difference that in *Pompée* there is no possibility of conversion, to be followed by marriage. César and Cléopâtre feel the injustice of a law that adheres to the letter and ignores the spirit of "Romanness" but have no clear plan of action for righting the wrong, other than reliance on César's persuasiveness in Rome:

CLÉOPÂTRE

Après tant de combats, je sais qu'un si grand homme
A droit de triompher des caprices de Rome,
Et que l'injuste horreur qu'elle eut toujours des rois
Peut céder par votre ordre à de plus justes lois.
Je sais que vous pouvez forcer d'autres obstacles;
Vous me l'avez promis, et j'attends ces miracles.
Votre bras dans Pharsale a fait de plus grands coups,
Et je ne les demande à d'autres Dieux qu'à vous.

CÉSAR

Tout miracle est facile où mon amour s'applique.

(4. 3. 1305–13)

The spectator knows that history will determine otherwise. Cléopâtre will await these miracles in vain; and it will take a god other than César to effect the new dispensation.[12]

We have seen that by detaining Cornélie in Egypt for a short while, Corneille is able to create, in the Lucan story of civil war, an interlude that he develops in an anti-Lucan way. New themes, new character traits—Cornélie's leap of faith, César's love (surpassing his heroic wrath), his desire to fight for Cléopâtre's right to be recognized as Roman—all turn the original story inside out. The "inserted" story, of Tassoan inspiration, is not brought to completion, however; and, as Barnwell has pointed out (pp. 201–3), frustration and failure lie at the heart of the play's action. César wants to prove his *générosité* toward Pompée, but the Egyptians deprive him of the chance. He wants to save Ptolomée, but an accident decides otherwise. He and Cléopâtre want to get married, but, as the audience knows, they will not be allowed to do so. The interlude in which Cornélie is free to admire the virtues of César must come to an end and give way again to the imperative to hate. History constantly acts in the play to impose limitations on the characters' noble impulses and so creates a pervasive air of inconclusiveness.[13] The lack of dramatic incident that has been noted in *Pompée* arises, in all probability, not so much from the failure of things to happen as from the failure of conflicts to be resolved, one way or another, with the accustomed sense of finality. The shifting tonalities of the play point up still further this strange incompleteness. The "negative" languages of irony, sarcasm, and cynicism are particularly strong in act 1, where Ptolomée is the central figure, but they continue to be heard throughout the play, competing in constantly varying patterns with a range of more "positive" languages extending from stoical proclamation to amorous hyperbole to tentative expressions of faith or wishful thinking. Only *Nicomède* comes close to showing a like richness of tone but with a much greater tendency toward sustained passages of one kind or another. In its language as in its action, *Pompée* remains in a perpetual state of flux.

How to judge this absence of definite resolution is our final problem here.[14] Were it not for *L'Illusion comique* and *Polyeucte*, one might posit the possibility of miscalculation on the author's part. That is, one could imagine that he set out to rectify the *Pharsalia* and discovered too late that the historical facts and characters were too well known to allow him to adapt them completely to a modern, Tassoan mold. Corneille's experience with the rectification of *Médée* and of book 4 of the *Aeneid* renders such a hypothesis untenable, however. He knew very well that unacknowledged rectification offered the only assurance of complete freedom to refashion an old subject. One must assume, accordingly, that the playwright deliberately intended to create the "failure" of *Pompée* and ask why he did so. The answer, I think, is that he wanted to convey the feeling of what it must have been like to live outside the realm of Providence. Dante, in *De Monarchia*, had broadened the idea of Providence to make it cover all of Roman history, the better to advance his own argument for the revival of the empire in Christian Europe. In the *Commedia*, however, he had recognized an unbridgeable gulf between the pagan and the Christian worlds and had shown Beatrice replacing Vergil as the pilgrim's guide. Closer to the time of *Pompée*, La Mothe le Vayer, in his treatise *De la vertu des payens* (1641), had again, but from a perspective totally different from that of the *De Monarchia*, raised the problem of the essential likeness or unlikeness of the pagan and Christian experiences. Corneille seems to have designed *Pompée* to reaffirm the importance of essential *differences*, perhaps in reaction to this treatise. From the orthodox Christian point of view (the view of Tasso and of the *Commedia*) a few pagans may have been privileged to play important roles in the slowly unfolding scheme of Providence; but for most pagans, no matter how illustrious, no matter how virtuous, history was less kind. They could strive to understand, happen on isolated spiritual insights, and come close to, but never really grasp, the ultimate truths. They were looking at the world as through a glass, darkly. The heroes of *Pompée* are exceptionally illustrious, but none of them enjoys the providential support of earlier Romans heroes in *Horace* and *Cinna*. We can admire Cornélie for her stoicism and for her desire to avenge her husband's murder, but we admire her more for her leap of faith and wish only that her willingness to believe could be met by a world that somehow sustained her belief better. César and Cléopâtre we admire for their exercise of power (connected with wrath) and for their *générosité*, but still more for their groping toward a conception of justice unknown even in Rome, the center of all known virtue. These characters have good impulses that they are powerless to transfer into action. It is as if they were waiting for a revelation that they have no way of knowing is actually coming or longing for the new dispensation that would give full meaning to their lives. Pompée's murder is as pathetic as Polyeucte's, but it lacks illumination and transcendency; Pompée is a martyr without a faith that could give meaning to his martyrdom, and in death he still casts an angry look at the gods. Throughout the play the Tassoan elements in *Pompée* seem to imply possibilities about to be realized, whereas the historical framework borrowed from Lucan suggests instead, at every turn, the limited possibilities of a world before the Redemption.

A kind of paralysis hangs over the action of the play, which is much more meditative than dramatic. To be sure, things happen, but, typically, by accident or in vain or counter to the "heroes' " expectations or desires. No one hero dominates the action from beginning to end; no single heroic will asserts itself fully and conclusively anywhere in the play. As if to emphasize the feeling of stasis, Corneille resorts to a number of long *récits* of offstage events and, in untypical fashion, makes no attempt to render them dramatic, does not have them delivered to a vitally interested party who will then react to, or act on, the information contained in the *récit*. The aim of the *récits* is apparently to induce, both in the onstage listener and in the audience, a grave reflectiveness, above all on the meaning of death. On this score, too, the play leads deliberately to an impasse. Pompée's death, I have said, lacks transcendency. In act 5, when his earthly remains are brought to Cornélie, she tries desperately to infuse a higher meaning into the terrible happenings, all to no avail. She speaks of her slain husband as a demigod and wants to place victims on his altar; and in a grotesque parody of Christian symbolism, she hopes to inspire Pompée's troops with the visible remains of his body:

> Je veux que de ma haine ils [les soldats] reçoivent des règles,
> Qu'ils suivent au combat des urnes au lieu d'aigles;
> Et que ce triste objet porte à leur souvenir
> Les soins de le venger, et ceux de te [= César] punir.
> (5. 4. 1713–16)

The audience knows that the cross on which Christ died would in time succeed in lifting the hearts of men in battle, not for the satisfaction of personal goals, but for the reconquest of the Holy City. Cornélie, however, left to her own, purely human devices, cannot conceive of so magnificent an undertaking.

At the end of the play, on the other hand, the death of Ptolomée is recounted, very curiously, in almost providential terms. Cornélie and César at different times both refer to the king's death as a sign of divine judgment:

> Le ciel règle souvent les effets par les causes,
> Et rend aux criminels ce qu'ils ont mérité.
> (5. 2. 1594–95)

> Prenez-vous-en au ciel, dont les ordres sublimes
> Malgré nos efforts savent punir les crimes.
> (5. 5. 1781–82)

Cléopâtre, for her part, had hoped in this case not for justice but for mercy:

> Comme de la justice, il [le ciel] a de la bonté.
> . . . .
> Souvent de la justice il passe à la douceur.
> (5. 2. 1596–99)

Ptolomée is ennobled somewhat by the brave manner of his death and by these attempts to connect it to some higher cause. But neither his death nor that of the hero Pompée is in fact ever redeemed in the full Christian sense. In death as in life, both hero and antihero can only manifest the void of a world before the coming of Christ.

La Mort de Pompée is Corneille's fourth Roman play in succession, but it is linked to the preceding trilogy only in the manner of an addendum. *Horace, Cinna,* and *Polyeucte* focus on the presence of Providence in the history of Rome, *Pompée* on its absence. *Horace, Cinna,* and *Polyeucte* utilize a dramaturgy that, at the denouement, opens onto reconciliation; *Pompée* shows a dramaturgy leading only to the sad persistence of original dichotomies. In the trilogy Corneille may have been drawn to the extreme synthetic views of Dante not so much because he meant to "correct" Tasso as because, under Tasso's influence, he was involved in a poetical undertaking that demanded the utmost in the way of synthesis. He was, I propose, trying to create a kind of summum of all previous heroic literature. Dante's summation of all Roman history under the auspices of Providence bespoke the same kind of extreme effort and, transferred into the plays, allowed Corneille to write about the same kind of high adventure that he himself was engaged in as he wrote.

Once the summation was done, there was obviously no point in doing it over, however. Corneille could only move on to something else, even though that something else would be bound to be an anticlimax. The sadness of *Pompée* probably reflects, in part, the playwright's realization that the glory of his theater, the highest heroic moment in his creative life, already lay in the past. Like Horace, he had outlived himself; like the Romans of *Pompée* he was reduced now to experiencing an absence of the "right" (poetical) situation. One must not, however, dwell too much on this idea, for fear it will obscure other truths of equal importance. *Pompée* is not only reflective, even self-reflective, but also imaginative and innovative. Long before Beckett, Corneille discovered that one could write an absorbing play in which not much happens, in which the point is that nothing much can happen. And he again showed himself capable of emulating Tasso by going a step farther than Tasso and becoming even more a modernist that his great predecessor. Tasso had implied that the modern poet had a choice between treating an ancient subject from the point of view of the Ancients—an exercise in literary archeology—or treating a Christian subject from the Christian point of view. Corneille found these alternatives too simple. In *Horace* and *Cinna* he had approached pagan Rome, probably through Dante, as a chapter in the history of Christendom. In *Pompée* he returned to pagan Rome to meditate, as a Christian, on the emptiness that lay at the center of its grandeur or, better, to contemplate its grave striving toward an illumination that only God could really provide. The Christian idea of Providence—through its presence or its absence—permitted him, he saw, to bring any subject into the domain of heroic Christian poetry.

CHAPTER VI
Théodore and *Héraclius*: Tasso, the Playwright

AFTER *POMPEE* CORNEILLE WROTE, FIRST, TWO COMEDIES around the figure of the liar, then, a group of three tragedies notable, among other things, for the prominence they give to protagonists of evil. All five works can be seen as, in part, reactions to the preceding Roman plays, and most particularly to the trilogy. The liar and the monster of evil, in different ways, are both counterparts to the providential heroes of Rome's greatness.

The theme of lying, which Corneille treats in *Le Menteur*, was by no means new in his theater. On the contrary, it had played an important role in every one of his early comedies, from *Mélite* to *L'Illusion comique*. But just as the rectification that he had practiced in *L'Illusion* became more deliberate after the Quarrel of the *Cid*, so his interest in lying seems to have been sharpened by the literary controversy and the subsequent writing of the Roman plays. Corneille's critics had attacked the *Cid* as a fraud, all glittery surface with no real substance; and Corneille, as we have seen, responded finally by constructing his next plays around the double truths of Roman history and the Christian faith. Polyeucte, the perfect hero, is an iconoclast and martyr who goes to his death proclaiming public witness to his newfound God. *Le Menteur* reverses the polarities of *Polyeucte*, substituting comedy for tragedy, and a liar for a truth-teller. *La Suite du Menteur*, in which the liar, Dorante, is reformed and begins to tell the truth, would seem to be, on the other hand, an effort to rectify comedy; that is, to test the premise just established in *Le Menteur* and to see whether the comic hero, like the earlier tragic hero, could not also be made into an ally of truth. If Corneille's intentions were indeed to reverse *Polyeucte* in *Le Menteur* and then correct *Le Menteur* in the *Suite*, the failure of the sequel apparently discouraged him from wanting to pursue further lines of development in the comic genre; and, with *Rodogune*, he returned to tragedy.

Rodogune, Théodore, and *Héraclius* make up a triad of plays second in importance in Corneille's theater only to *Horace, Cinna*, and *Polyeucte*. Couton refers to them collectively as "la trilogie des monstres" (p. 112), Sweetser as "les pièces manichéennes" (p. 138). They compose a trilogy only in the very loosest sense. From Cléopâtre to Marcelle to Phocas one can see, it is true, a gradual decline from an absolute of monstrosity, just as earlier one saw in Horace, Auguste, and Polyeucte a gradual ascent toward ever higher levels of heroic virtue. This new gradation exists in something of a vacuum, however. It is not linked to any step-by-step unfolding of a central historical vision, is not integrated into any other grander pattern of ethical or cultural evolution. As a consequence, the considerable difference visible between the almost totally monstrous Cléopâtre of *Rodogune* and the rather human Phocas of *Héraclius* is apt to strike one, if at all, as merely accidental. The plays do, however, all evince the same general dramatic structure: marked by the clear-cut opposition of good and evil, and the attendant double reversal at the denouement. This formula is basically the Tassoan formula of *Pompée*, minus the complicating admixture of Lucan and the *Pharsalia*. Corneille has emphasized the evil characters much more than Tasso ever intended, however. He has also drastically narrowed the scope of the action and, instead of focussing on conflicts of worldwide import, deals now with disputes that scarcely go beyond the walls of a single palace, or the concern of a single royal family. These two adjustments in all probability are not independent of each other. In the Roman plays, Corneille had already shown virtue playing itself out on the grand stage of Roman history. Could he now, in the new group of plays, do something of the same thing for evil? Theoretically, yes; but in fact it would have gone against his grain for the playwright to unleash evil on the full arena of world politics. By reducing the range of influence of his evil characters, however, he could contain or neutralize their evil to some extent. I am suggesting, in other words, that the sacrifice of epic scope was the price that Corneille had to pay in order to feel free elsewhere to amplify greatly the role of his antiheroes.

The "monster" plays, like the "liar" plays, appear then, to represent modulations whose negativity the playwright seeks to contain. An essential element of this containment can be seen in the playwright's continued interest in rectification. For it is not only *La Suite du Menteur* that sets out to correct the flaws of an earlier text; *Rodogune, Théodore,* and *Héraclius* have this aim also. Marc Fumaroli (in his article, "Tragique païen et tragique chrétien dans *Rodogune*") has clearly demonstrated the complexity of the various corrections implied in the text of the first of Corneille's "monster" plays; and I have nothing to add to what he has already said so well. To my knowledge, no one, however, has noticed or commented on a series of concealed rectifications central to *Théodore* and *Héraclius.* The purpose of this chapter will be to study these other rectifications, which have the added interest for us in the present context of being carried out on the only two dramatic texts that Tasso himself has left us: the dramatic pastoral, *Aminta,* and the tragedy, *Torrismondo.*

THÉODORE AND *AMINTA*

At first glance hagiography and pastoral poetry would appear to have little or nothing in common, and indeed it will be my argument here that Corneille wanted to keep the two genres apart. By the time the playwright came to treat it, however, the story of Saint Theodora had acquired—together with an allegorical meaning that I shall examine in a later chapter—a well-developed love interest where none had existed originally. Saint Ambrose, whom Corneille cites as a source, recounts that Theodora, after being cast in a brothel for refusal to recant, was rescued from her predicament by the intervention of a Christian *frater,* Didymus, at whose side she was later martyred. No mention is made of love. In the play of Girolamo Bartolommei, which scholars often suggest as a more recent source for Corneille, Theodora, though of course still a Christian virgin, has become a "ninfa" in the eyes of Christian and pagan characters alike; and

Didymus is only one among several suitors for her hand.[1] Between these extremes lie several other Italian plays on the subject and also the Olindo-Sophronia episode in Tasso's *Gerusalemme liberata* (2. 32), which, Fumaroli has pointed out, is both pastoral in tone and modeled on the second half of the saint's story (where Theodora and Didymus contend with each other for the glory of a martyr's death).[2]

If in our imagination we superimpose the text of Corneille's *Théodore* on the text of Tasso's *Aminta*, we can readily perceive several important concordances. In both works we find a respectful hero in pursuit of a virginal heroine with whom he is finally united. The heroine begins by rejecting her suitor rather roughly, but eventually yields to his importunities. And the young hero, in both cases, rescues the virgin from a brutal sexual assault planned by another. The nature of the love involved is quite different in the two texts, as are the circumstances of the lovers' final union. *Aminta* is a celebration of youth's awakening to the delights of love, including the excitement of the senses. *Théodore*, on the other hand, aims at the suppression of the senses and a sublimation of human love into the all-embracing love of God. The satyr who attacks Silvia at the fountain, like the coarse soldiers who would violate Théodore in the brothel, represents the degradation of love into animalistic lust. But over against this nightmare image of love, the *Aminta*, which ends with the lovers' marriage, evokes the vision of lawful, human sensual bliss, whereas *Théodore* unites the couple only in a martyrdom undertaken above all for the love of God. These are differences of tone or of coloring, however; they do not invalidate the basic homology of the plots, the harmony of the basic structural patterns.

To note these similarities in plot incident does not, of course, prove that Corneille himself necessarily was aware of them. The parallels might be construed as accidental or at least inadvertent on the playwright's part, something he inherited perhaps from earlier versions of Theodora's life. In fact, however, Corneille seems not only to have seen the homologies but wanted us to know he had seen them.

Let us start with Didyme, Théodore's suitor, later her savior, and finally her co-martyr. Didyme is mentioned as a suitor early in the play, notably in act 2, scene 2, where the heroine confesses to her cousin Cléobule that, if she were to marry anyone, it would be Didyme. She has rejected him and intends to continue rejecting him—for reasons that for the moment she withholds, but that involve a secret vow to save her love for God alone. She feels attracted to Didyme, however, and must struggle with herself to resist him:

> [Oui, j'aimerois Didyme,]
> Didyme, que sur tous je tâche d'éloigner,
> Et qui verroit bientôt sa flamme couronnée,
> Si mon âme à mes sens étoit abandonnée,
> Et se laissoit conduire à ces impressions
> Que forment en naissant les belles passions.

Théodore's understanding of her own emotions is quite sophisticated—too much so, perhaps, to be entirely plausible. One suspects that the playwright, here and in what follows, is sacrificing strict verisimilitude for purposes of defining as clearly as possible his own ideological stance, which is antipastoral. For what the heroine analyzes in herself and tries, through analysis, to transcend is obviously the traditional pastoral conception of love, familiar to Corneille's audiences through both novels and theater.

> Mais comme enfin c'est lui qu'il faut que plus je craigne,
> Plus je penche à l'aimer, et plus je le dédaigne,
> Et m'arme d'autant plus que mon coeur en secret
> Voudroit s'en laisser vaincre, et combat à regret.

This psychology would apply as well to Silvia as to Théodore, but Tasso's heroine is much too naïve and untutored to be able to analyze it for herself:

> Je me fais tant d'effort, lorsque je le méprise,
> Que par mes propres sens je crains d'être surprise;
> J'en crains une révolte, et que las d'obéir
> Comme je les trahis, ils ne m'osent trahir.
>
> (2. 2. 390–402)

Elsewhere in the early acts of the play, Didyme is also presented to us indirectly through a rival, Placide, the Roman governor's son, who is also in love with Théodore. In the opening scene of the play, Placide complains of the cruel treatment he has received from Théodore and attributes it to a supposed preference on her part for Didyme:

> Sans doute elle aime ailleurs, et s'impute à bonheur
> De préférer Didyme au fils du gouverneur.
>
> (1. 1. 93–94)

His confidant—Cléobule again—replies that Didyme is in fact not lucky either:

> Ce malheureux rival dont vous êtes jaloux
> En reçoit chaque jour plus de mépris que vous.
>
> (1. 1. 101–2)

Didyme's entrance onstage—as distinct from mentions made about him earlier—is delayed until very late in the play, until the last scene of act 4. When he finally appears, we see him win out over Placide in their contest for Théodore. For it is he, not Placide, who has rescued the maiden from the brothel; and Placide himself ends up recognizing his rival's supremacy and voluntarily withdraws (4. 5). Then, in act 5, we see Didyme finally win acceptance of a sort from Théodore, as the malevolent Marcelle consigns them both to a shared martyrdom:

> THÉODORE, *à Didyme*
> Ainsi de ce combat que la vertu nous donne,
> Nous sortirons tous deux avecque la couronne.
>
> DIDYME
> Oui, Madame, on exauce et vos voeux et les miens;
> Dieu. . . .
>
> MARCELLE
> Vous suivrez ailleurs de si doux entretiens.
> Amenez-les tous deux.
>
> (5. 6. 1715–19)

Didyme, I have said, makes his initial appearance on stage at the end of act 4. By that time he has been arrested for helping Théodore escape and is led in by a guard. Cléobule catches sight of him as he approaches and, turning to Placide, says the following:

> Le voici qu'Amyntas vous amène à main-forte.
>
> (4. 4. 1367)

Amyntas, the guard, has no lines to speak and no other function in the play than to usher in Didyme when Didyme appears for the first time. Conceivably the name could be without significance. Another guard, in *Héraclius*, will also be called Amyntas. But here in *Théodore*, in conjunction with a hero whose role, we have seen, is parallel to that of Aminta, the name is more likely to be the playwright's way of acknowledging the two heroes' filiation.

Let us turn now to Théodore. The world of Corneille's play contains a wider spectrum of amorous possibilities than the *Aminta*, where, besides virginity, the only options for Silvia are union with the satyr (lust) or union with Aminta (marriage). Théodore has not only these two options but two other, higher ones as well—spiritual union with a mortal (Didyme) and spiritual union with God.[3] The plot describes the proposals and counterproposals, the rejections and choices by which the heroine finally accedes to the highest of all these stages of love. Théodore's two suitors both offer her a way out of her terrible predicament—Placide just before, Didyme just after, she is sent to the brothel. Placide proposes an escape to Egypt and eventual marriage; Didyme, an exchange of clothes that will allow the maiden to escape the brothel alone while he remains behind to be arrested in her place. On both occasions Théodore begins by resisting the offer and proposing instead that her suitor solve her problem either by killing her or by providing her the means to kill herself. Both men, of course, refuse her bizarre request, thereby forcing Théodore to come to terms as best she can with their original offers, aided always by her faith in the providence of God. In the first instance, she categorically rejects the idea of marriage to Placide, in terms that foreshadow the next, higher option that Didyme will soon offer her:

Vous n'êtes pas celui dont Dieu s'y veut servir:
Il saura bien sans vous en susciter un autre,
Dont le bras moins puissant, mais plus saint que le vôtre,
Par un zèle plus pur se fera mon appui,
Sans porter ses desirs sur un bien tout à lui.

(3. 3. 946–50)

In the second instance, she hesitates, not because Didyme is demanding anything like marriage in return for having rescued her, but because she can escape only by leaving Didyme to suffer arrest in her stead. As Didyme relates the incident in act 4, what resolved the dilemma for Théodore was the belief—illumination?—that it was God's will that she take this means to avoid enforced prostitution:

> Je m'apprête à l'échange, elle à la mort s'apprête;
> Je lui tends mes habits, elle m'offre sa tête,
> Et demande à sauver un si précieux bien
> Aux dépens de son sang, plutôt qu'au prix du mien;
> Mais Dieu la persuade, et notre combat cesse.
> Je vois, suivant mes voeux, échapper la Princesse.
>
> (4. 4. 1447−52)

A second "combat" is engaged between the couple, this time on stage, in act 5, when Théodore unexpectedly surrenders herself to the authorities (claiming that God has told her meanwhile that she will now not be placed back in the brothel, but rather martyred). In a reversal of the situation earlier inside the brothel, it is now she who proposes to die in place of Didyme, and it is now Didyme who resists. The providential solution is supplied this time through Marcelle, who determines to send them to death together. Théodore, like Silvia but on a higher ethical level, relents and accepts this shared martyrdom with Didyme: "Ainsi de ce combat que la vertu nous donne,/Nous sortirons tous deux avecque la couronne." And Didyme, for his part, is more than satisfied to be joined with Théodore, not in earthly marriage, but in a common union with God: "Oui, Madame, on exauce et vos voeux et les miens" (l. 1717). The denouement is a rectified, Christian version of the pastoral denouement of the *Aminta.*

That these parallels might be accidental or unconscious would seem to be denied by a curious exchange early in act 5 between Didyme and Cléobule. Didyme is under arrest and is awaiting his sentence of death. Far from being saddened by the prospect, he is overjoyed; death will ensure him a martyr's crown and eternal happiness in heaven. Cléobule, Didyme's friend as well as Théodore's cousin, urges another scenario with quite different implications. Théodore, he says, is hiding in his house. What is more, he insinuates that she is now ready to marry her Christian suitor, out of gratitude for what he did to save her from the brothel:

CLÉOBULE

Il faut vivre, Didyme, il faut vivre.

DIDYME

Et j'y cours.
Pour la cause de Dieu s'offrir en sacrifice,
C'est courir à la vie, et non pas au supplice.

CLÉOBULE

Peut-être dans ta secte est-ce une vision;
Mais l'heur que je t'apporte est sans illusion.
Théodore est à toi: ce dernier témoignage
Et de ta passion et de ton grand courage
A si bien en amour changé tous ses mépris,
Qu'elle t'attend chez moi pour t'en donner le prix.

(5. 3. 1546–54)

What Cléobule describes here is the ordinary pastoral denouement wherein, as in the *Aminta*, the maiden finally yields to her
suitor's demands in recognition of proofs he has given of his
devotion to her. There is no reason to believe that Théodore has
in fact entertained any of the notions put forth here by Cléobule.
On the contrary, as soon as she discovers that Didyme has been
arrested, she rushes to the palace to give herself up. Cléobule's
proposal functions as a means of showing the superior strength
of character and the higher intentions of Didyme. It shows him
to be, morally speaking, superior to Aminta. And Didyme's steadfast rejection serves in turn to distance Corneille and the play he
is writing from all the earthly pleasures that count for so much in
the pastoral tradition:

Va, dangereux ami que l'enfer me suscite,
Ton damnable artifice en vain me sollicite:
Ce coeur, inébranlable aux plus cruels tourments,
A presque été surpris de tes chatouillements;
Leur mollesse a plus fait que le fer ni la flamme:
Elle a frappé mes sens, elle a brouillé mon âme;
Ma raison s'est troublée, et mon foible a paru;
Mais j'ai dépouillé l'homme, et Dieu m'a secouru.

(5. 3. 1579–86)

The "weakness" that Cléobule assumes will motivate the
actions of both Théodore and Didyme is the "weakness" that
pastoral poetry has as its very purpose to celebrate. In rejecting it,
or in rising above it, through his two saintly characters, Corneille

rectifies the pastoral in general and the *Aminta* in particular. This is not to say, of course, that the playwright wished to condemn love and earthly marriage once and for all. Corneille was not himself a saint; nor was he interested in writing only about the saintly, as his later theater proves beyond all doubt. As I have suggested, however, he did want to measure himself against Tasso, and that emulation necessarily involved the attempt to advance beyond Tasso just as Tasso had advanced beyond Vergil. In the context of such an emulation, it would make sense for Corneille, in *Théodore*, to use a saint's story to rectify the pastoral *Aminta*. Tasso, in the *Discorsi*, had advocated the choice of a Christian subject and a perfect hero, but only for epic poetry. Corneille, we saw earlier, went beyond Tasso when, in *Polyeucte*, he introduced a perfect hero into tragedy. Similarly, if I am not mistaken, he wanted to Christianize the pastoral, as Tasso before him had Christianized the epic. And to make his accomplishment even more pointed, he chose to recall and reject the *Aminta* within the very framework of the Christian tragedy of *Théodore*.[4]

There remains another homology that we need to consider, one having to do not with character or plot but rather with mode of presentation: namely, the use by both Tasso and Corneille of dramatic narration to convey the events surrounding the hero's rescue of the heroine. Taking the whole of the plays into account, one would have to say that in this case the homology is quite partial. For Tasso employs narration as a device throughout the *Aminta*, whereas Corneille restricts its use in effect to act 4. The narrated actions in the *Aminta* include, besides the incidents at the fountain, such incidents as Silvia's encounter with a wolf and Aminta's leap off a cliff. All these actions are inherently less stageable, from a practical point of view, than Théodore's incarceration in, and escape from, the brothel. The most important difference between the two plays, insofar as narration is concerned, centers, however, on the writers' attitudes toward narration, more particularly on their view of how narration fits into their overall aesthetic scheme. Tasso, it would seem, uses the device, and uses it frequently, primarily because he found that it blended in perfectly with the lyrical, reflective tone of the whole pastoral. Corneille, on the other hand, as one sees from his remarks in the Examen, would have preferred actually to show the scenes in the brothel and fell back on narration as a necessary concession to *bienséance*.

The place of the *Aminta* in the history of *bienséance* is rather ambiguous. Guarini had taken Tasso to task for his too complaisant exaltation of sensual love,[5] yet by Corneille's time, in France, the *Aminta* itself was being praised for its exemplary decency. Tasso profited in France from comparison with his early French translators and adaptors, most of whom failed to appreciate the lyricism of the *Aminta* and proceeded, presumably in the name of greater dramatic effectiveness, to turn the narration of the fountain scene into staged action with dialogue. In the process Tasso's delicacy and tact had been lost. The versions of Fonteny, Belliard, Du Mas, Rayssiguier, and Quinet (?) all took this route and constituted a well-established tradition.[6] Vion d'Alibray, an ally and possibly also a friend of Corneille's, broke with this tradition in 1632 and published a translation of the *Aminta* that made a point of restoring the narrations found in the original. In the Advertissement, which is one of the most enlightening of the period, d'Alibray not only praises the artistry of Tasso but, especially as regards the narrations, commends him also for his sense of decorum:

> . . . Il est bon de soustraire à la cõnaissance de la veuë beaucoup de choses qui sont incontinent apres suffisamment racontées. C'est pourquoy on ne sçauroit assez loüer la modestie du Tasse de nous avoir caché l'insolence du Satyre & la nudité de Sylvie: Ce que l'honnesteté l'ayant contraint de faire, il ne pouvoit par consequent nous faire voir le coup dont Aminte s'alloit tuer sans le secours de Daphné. . . . Ioint que cette action de desespoir d'Aminte estoit de mauvais exemple pour le peuple, devant qui, comme un grand maistre a dit, il ne faut pas que Médée tue ses enfans. . . . (No pagination)

Tasso's extensive use of narrations in the *Aminta*, as I have said, probably arose from other than ethical concerns. Still, d'Alibray's remarks and the history of the pastoral's translations in France provide a useful context in which to look at Corneille's own use of narrations in *Théodore*. For if, as is likely, the playwright thought that he was ensuring the decorum of his play by resorting to narration of the events in the brothel, then he made a rather serious miscalculation. For in fact act 4 succeeds only in subverting the purity that the other acts of *Théodore* make such a

point of establishing. Tasso devotes one long speech to rehears-
ing the events at the fountain. Corneille extends the narration of
the scene in the brothel over most of a whole act. In order to
make the narrations more effective dramatically, moreover, he
distributes them among three different narrators—Paulin, Cléobule, and Didyme—who appear in ascending order of the importance of their information and of their closeness to Théodore. None of them anticipates the conclusion of the events,
which serves to create suspense. Moreover, the narrations and
the suspense they generate are directed at a vitally interested
character, Placide. In fact, because Placide's honor is said to be
linked directly to the fate of his beloved, the anguish that he
experiences as he listens impatiently to the gradual unfolding of
the story parallels the anguish that the virgin herself must have
suffered but that Corneille could not show. The "diverses agita-
tions" and the "troubles" that the playwright had so admired in
Saint Ambrose's telling of the story in *De Virginibus*, through
sophisticated use of narrations, has been transferred to Placide
(whose name must surely be intended as ironic and counter-
characterial, like that of Sévère). Act 4 is a miracle of technical
virtuosity, and Corneille was in a way right to take pride in it in
the Examen. He obtains this superior dramatic effectiveness at
the expense of sacrificing restraint, however. For though he
never depicts anything offensive—in fact, nothing offensive ever
actually occurs in the brothel—he does show Placide repeatedly
tormented by suspicions of the worst sort and frustrated at not
having been able to prevent the presumed violation of Théodore. Dramatic it certainly is, but act 4 verges also on indecency,
an indecency born, ironically, of an obsession with avoiding the
indecent. The play purports to provide a kind of Christian rectification of the *Aminta*, and to some extent it does. But in its most
striking part it succeeds only in reducing the ordeal of a virgin
saint to an occasion for prurience.[7]

HÉRACLIUS AND *TORRISMONDO*

Héraclius bears much the same relation to *Torrismondo* as
Théodore does to the *Aminta*, except that the parallels in this
instance are of a somewhat more general nature. In fact, were it
not for what we already know of Corneille's sustained effort to
emulate the accomplishments of his great Italian predecessor,

the links between *Héraclius* and *Torrismondo* would probably not be construable as really significant. We are not approaching *Héraclius* as an isolated phenomenon, however, but as another, the last, in a series of related phenomena all of which in some way or another we can read as rectifications of or through Tasso.

With this in mind, let us begin by noting that the subjects of both plays for all practical purposes are invented. Both playwrights make obeisance in the direction of historicity, Tasso by designating his principal characters as members of the ruling families of several Scandinavian kingdoms, Corneille by preserving the real imperial succession linking Tibère to Maurice and Maurice, by way of the usurper Phocas, to Héraclius. D'Alibray, who also translated *Torrismondo*, credits Tasso's play with an "intrigue de Roman," and, as evidence of its lack of historical basis, points out that, between the first and the final versions, Tasso had reversed the nature of the relationship between the friends, Torrismondo and Germondo, making Torrismondo into a betrayer of friendship, whereas he had originally been the victim of betrayal. Corneille, for his part, readily confessed that *Héraclius* contained "encore plus d'efforts d'invention que . . . *Rodogune*," a play that, as he had already indicated, made very short shrift of historical fact. Indeed, he looked on *Héraclius* as something of a *cas limite*, whose success should not, he thought, be taken as encouragement to proceed further in the same direction: "C'est beaucoup hasarder, et l'on n'est pas toujours heureux; et dans un dessein de cette nature, ce qu'un bon succès fait passer pour une ingénieuse hardiesse, un mauvais le fait prendre pour une témérité ridicule" (Au Lecteur).

Both plays also have plots that deal with a double substitution of infants and a series of ensuing complications years later, a type of plot popular in the theater and novel of the time, but one that Corneille himself had never exploited before. Alvida and Rosmonda, in the Italian play, have grown up in ignorance of their true identities. Alvida is assumed to be a Norwegian princess; in reality she was only adopted by the king of Norway following the death of his own daughter. The king of Norway had gotten the child from pirates, who had stolen her from agents of her real father. Alvida's real father had set all these developments in motion by sending his own daughter away from the the palace and, in her place, substituting the daughter of a nurse—all in hopes of avoiding a dire fate predicted by a nymph. The child he brought up as his own is known as Rosmonda. The real Rosmonda, however, is Alvida. The play involves in part the way in which the identities of these two women are sorted out.

Corneille's plot for *Héraclius* assumes a similar set of exchanges, but of male instead of female infants. Some twenty years before the play's opening, Phocas the tyrant killed the emperor Maurice and ordered that the emperor's infant son, Héraclius, also be put to death. In order to frustrate this heinous plan, a gentlewoman, Léontine, had played a complicated double trick on the tyrant. First, she substituted her own son for Héraclius, allowing her own child to be murdered in order to save the future emperor. As an added precaution, she managed later to exchange Héraclius for the tyrant's infant son, Martian. As a consequence of these switches, the young man whom Léontine has reared as a son is in fact the tyrant's son, and the young man who is presumed to be the tyrant's son is in reality Héraclius, the legitimate heir to the throne.

To the theme of mistaken identities, *Torrismondo* and *Héraclius* both also add the theme of incest. Torrismondo has traveled to Norway to bring Alvida back as a wife for his friend Germondo, but, like Tristan, has fallen in love with the woman himself. Indeed, on the trip home, the lovers have consummated their passion. Torrismondo's guilt is increased upon discovery later that Alvida is the real Rosmonda, thus his own sister. Corneille, for his part, stops short of actual incest and, instead, merely flirts with the idea of it. On the other hand, he adds the related themes of threatened parricide and infanticide. For at one time or another in the play, the action is headed in the direction of Héraclius's being married to Pulchérie, his sister; of Phocas's possibly killing his own son in ignorance of his identity; and finally of Phocas's real son thinking he is the emperor's son and planning to kill the tyrant, actually his father. As the foregoing partial summaries indicate, the plots of these plays are immensely complicated—so much so, apparently, that audiences found them difficult to follow. D'Alibray's translation, *Torrismon*, was produced at the Marais in 1635, with Montdory taking the title role, to great popular acclaim.[8] In spite of this success in the theater, d'Alibray refers over and over to the excessive complication of the plot. In the preface to the published text, he confesses not to have liked the play himself at first and says he came to admire it only later on when he had mastered the surface confusion. In order to help the spectators at the Marais, he had deleted certain unnecessary details in the original; and for the readers of *Torrismon* he supplies both a prefatory Argument and, in the text of the play, explanatory marginal comments as well. Whether one approached the play in the theater or through reading—and d'Alibray says he doubts Tasso ever intended it to be staged—it posed serious problems, as do all such works of great intricacy of plot. The danger, he says, is that the spectator or reader will be too busy deciphering the story line to experience any tragic emotion: "Il peut arriver que [de telles oeuvres] travaillent davantage nostre esprit pour les comprẽdre, que nous ne sommes emeus à compassion par les accidens qu'elles representent." The only remedy, d'Alibray concludes, is to do as he himself had done in the beginning and to see or read the play more than once.

Corneille's remarks on *Héraclius* often seem to echo d'Alibray's preface to *Torrismon*. He readily grants the over-complication of the plot and, by way of help to the reader, provides, not a whole summary, but a list of the essential true and assumed identities of the characters. In the Examen he comments briefly on the reaction of spectators to the play: "J'ai vu de fort bons esprits, et des personnes des plus qualifiées de la cour, se plaindre de ce que sa représentation fatiguoit autant l'esprit qu'une étude sérieuse." His conclusion, parallel to d'Alibray's, is that the only solution lies in repetition: "[La pièce] n'a pas laissé de plaire; mais je crois qu'il l'a fallu voir plus d'une fois pour en remporter une entière intelligence."

Rectification, I have said, involves two aspects: adopting a model, but then departing from it in some obvious way so as to correct it. Up to now we have seen only the elements that *Héraclius* can be said to have in common with *Torrismondo*: namely, a subject that is ostensibly historical but in fact totally invented; the related themes of mistaken identity, caused by a double substitution of infants and resulting in the commission or threatened commission of such horrible crimes as incest, parricide, and infanticide; and, finally, an attendant critical commentary that stresses the great complexity of the plot and its effect on audiences. What remains to be seen is how, in the context of these likenesses, *Héraclius* can be seen to "improve" upon *Torrismondo*, its presumed model.

The plot of *Torrismondo* suffers from defects other than its elaborateness. According to d'Alibray, Tasso had erred in cramming an inordinate number of essential revelations into act 4; the uneven distribution of information throughout the play, he thought, only raised more problems for the reader or spectator. Corneille seems to have been conscious of just such a danger in writing *Héraclius*, and in the Examen he explains how he sought to meet it: "[Les narrations] sont éparses ici dans tout le poëme, et ne font connoître à la fois que ce qu'il est besoin qu'on sache pour l'intelligence de la scène qui suit." Another weakness of *Torrismondo* lies in its duplicity of action. The first three acts are built around Torrismondo's guilt at having betrayed his friend Germondo and his indecision about what course to take when Germondo arrives. Not only has he fallen in love with his friend's intended bride; he has slept with her also. What, in the circumstances, does he now owe his friend? Should he confess his crime? Or hand over Alvida as if nothing has happened? Or, perhaps, try to get Germondo to marry Rosmonda (Torrismondo's supposed sister) instead? Only in act 4 does the awful truth begin to emerge that Torrismondo's real sister is not Rosmonda but Alvida, so that his love for the latter constitutes not just a betrayal of friendship but, even more devastatingly, incest as well. The focus of the play shifts quite abruptly in this act, and with no forewarning Torrismondo, who appears first as a kind of male Phaedra, turns suddenly instead into a counterpart of Oedipus. Corneille, for all the complications of the plot he spins, is never in danger of violating unity of action in *Héraclius*. In place of Tasso's two themes of betrayal of friendship and incest, Corneille has three: incest, parricide, and infanticide; but whereas it is only accident that connects the two themes of *Torrismondo*, the three themes of *Héraclius* all derive from a single, central crux—the problem of obscure identity.

The most striking difference between the two plays lies, however, in the area of their conception of tragedy. *Torrismondo* corresponds perfectly to the views on the tragic genre expounded by Tasso himself in the *Discorsi*. The hero is of middling virtue: weak enough to covet his friend's fiancée, upstanding enough to feel guilt-ridden afterward. His fall is inevitable;

his father's attempts to avert the predictions of the nymph by abandoning his daughter only serve, ironically, to fulfill the predictions. It was fated that the royal line should be cut off; and at the end of the play, it is. Torrismondo and Alvida (actually Rosmonda), brother and sister, both kill themselves; and the throne of the Goths passes over to Germondo. *Héraclius* has to do with the fate of a royal line also, but the end result in this case is happy. For it is Providence, not fate, that prevails in Corneille's play. At the time of the emperor Maurice's murder at the hands of Phocas, Providence intervened, through Léontine, to conceal the identity of the heir, Héraclius, and so to save him. Twenty years later, when it is time for Héraclius to assert his rightful claim to the throne, and when ignorance of his true identity is on the verge of leading him into an incestuous marriage, Providence intervenes again to save him, this time by revealing who he really is. Léontine's word, inadequate by itself to guarantee the truth, is backed up, providentially, by the appearance of two crucial letters, one in the hand of the dead emperor, the other in that of his empress. (I am skipping over a number of vague premonitions said to come from "Dieu," "le ciel," or "la voix du sang.") In the end the good characters—that is, Héraclius, his sister Pulchérie, Léontine, and even the tyrant's son, whom Léontine has reared as her own—all survive, but Phocas, the evil tyrant, is killed. Through this double reversal at the denouement, the throne reverts, as it should, to Héraclius. *Torrismondo* adheres to the Tassoan conception of tragedy; *Héraclius*, obviously, to the Tassoan conception of epic poetry—transposed by Corneille to the genre of tragedy. This is not the first time that the French playwright so rectified the author of the *Discorsi.* In *Polyeucte* he had already appropriated for tragedy the perfect hero of epic, and, in *Pompée,* the epic's dichotomous world view and the plot with a double reversal, both advocated, but only for epic, by Tasso. What marks the rectification in *Héraclius* as unusual is the fact that, as in *Théodore,* it is carried out on a play of Tasso himself.

Corneille had made his real assault on Tasso's fame in the Roman trilogy, where he had borrowed from epic poetry in order to forge a new concept of tragedy. The use of this concept later on to rectify Tasso's two plays (after first rectifying *Electra* in *Rodogune*) does not in itself represent a major advance in the progress of poetry toward the goal of ultimate perfection. At most it serves only to validate or to reaffirm a position that the playwright had already laid claim to in earlier plays. As in the Roman trilogy, where the playwright and his heroes were both engaged in breaking through to new levels of truth, so here in the "trilogie des monstres" there is again a harmony between the playwright's own situation, *qua* poet, and that of his heroes. For the heroes of the later plays no longer make new discoveries in the realm of heroic decorum; like the playwright who created them and who, in doing so, seems to have projected his own present preoccupations onto them, they are already in possession of their greatness at the outset of the play and are intent not on adding to it but rather on just defending it.

By juxtaposing Tasso and Corneille as absolute opposites, Scudéry had inadvertently issued a challenge that the author of the *Cid* had first taken up in the dedicatory letter for *La Suivante* and that in time led to the much more important emulation of Tasso in the Roman trilogy. *Horace, Cinna,* and *Polyeucte* constitute the playwright's bold claim on the ultimate reaches of poetic fame; they are also his answer to, and his refutation of, the critics who had attacked him during the Quarrel. In writing the "trilogie des monstres," Corneille no longer had the same need for Tasso that he had had before. The purpose for which he had originally sought to emulate the Italian poet had been met and no longer existed; Corneille was free henceforth to think about other things than the Quarrel. That he continued nevertheless to be preoccupied with Tasso may be attributed to either or both of two reasons. The playwright may have wanted to rectify *Aminta* and *Torrismondo* simply out of a sense of gratitude to Tasso, to whom he knew he owed so much. He may, on the other hand, have felt that same gratitude as something of a burden and sought to reduce it by demonstrating as directly as possible his own superiority to Tasso, at least as a playwright. However that may be, it is likely, I think, that Corneille felt himself square with Tasso after *Héraclius,* just as after *Polyeucte* he had had reason to consider himself free of the critics who had hounded him during the Quarrel.

CHAPTER VII

Views of Poetry and the Poet

THE FOREGOING CHAPTERS HAVE TRIED TO SHOW HOW IT was that from *Horace* to *Héraclius* Corneille planned his career and articulated his plays in emulation of Torquato Tasso. Such extensive emulation implies an exceptionally high degree of poetical self-consciousness, for the playwright is constantly measuring his present play by the standard of some previous work, and his own accomplishment in writing it by the accomplishments of those greats who have preceded him, particularly Tasso. In this chapter I propose to look at Corneille's self-consciousness from two other angles: one still inside the plays, but at another level from that of the rectification of earlier literary texts; the other, in a major critical work, the "Discours de la tragédie." What we see from these two additional perspectives will, I hope, serve to confirm the coherence and the continuity of Corneille's inspiration from *Horace* to *Héraclius* and will suggest once more the crucial importance of Tasso and the Quarrel of the *Cid* to the elaboration of Corneille's modernist vision.

PART I: ALLEGORIES OF POETRY AND THE POET

The limits of allegory are not easy to define. The dialogue between Melpomène and Le Soleil in the prologue of *Andromède* surely qualifies, as does the more complex prologue of *La Toison d'or*, where Corneille assigns roles to La Victoire, Mars, La Paix, and La France, among others. The outer-frame play of *L'Illusion comique* develops a somewhat more subtle form of allegory, but one that still leaves no doubt as to an intended second meaning for the magician (he is the playwright) or for the magician's grotto (it is the theater). When Corneille elsewhere speaks of Cléopâtre (in *Rodogune*) as being a "seconde Médée," is he, by inviting us to view his heroine as at one and the same time herself and another, tending toward allegory? Is the little parody of *Médée* in act 5 of *L'Illusion,* by any stretch of the imagination, also an allegory? If so, then it is clear that Pauline, whose role rectifies those of Dido and Chimène and is thus both herself and two others, may also reveal allegorical aspects. In this final chapter, I shall aim at uncovering, within *Horace, Polyeucte,* and *Théodore,* what I think can legitimately be called a series of allegories, and if not always allegories, then at the very least extended metaphors, symbols, or images. They all have to do with the poet and poetry and, in one way or another, they all lead back to the Quarrel of the *Cid,* the formative event in Corneille's emergence as the dramatic poet we know today.

Horace *and the Allegory of the* Duellum

The Quarrel generated a number of allegories, by far the most important of which was the allegory of persecution. We shall have occasion later on to consider it in some detail. For now let us begin with the allegory of the *duellum,* which Chapelain proposed in the opening pages of the *Sentiments* as a means of countering the idea that the Academy was persecuting Corneille. Ideally, he says, literary dispute ought to be viewed as "une espece de guerre qui est avantageuse pour tous," as "une course, où celuy qui emporte le prix semble ne l'avoir poursuivy que pour en faire un present à son rival" (Gasté, p. 357). The prize, to be shared by all, would be deliverance from "l'inquietude des doutes," or, to put it more positively, the attainment of "cet agreable repos que [l'entendement humain] trouve dans la certitude des connoissances." The basic condition for a happy outcome of this sort is that the combatants should be "honnestes" and respect each other: "C'est une espece de guerre qui est avantageuse pour tous, lors qu'elle se fait civilement, et que les armes empoisonnées y sont defenduës." Chapelain does not use this allegory throughout; he begins by saying, in rather more straightforward fashion: "On peut mesme meriter de la loüange en donnant du blasme, pourveu que les reprehensions partent du zele de l'utilité commune, et qu'on ne pretende pas eslever sa reputation sur les ruines de celle d'autruy" (Gasté, p. 355). He resorts to allegory as a means of strengthening his argument. The allegory ennobles the idea of literary controversy by likening it to an idealized form of chivalric warfare. And when he alludes to Tasso and Guarini, it is not only as literary figures, but also, by implication, as knights: "En effect nous en avons la principale obligation aux agreables differens qu'ont produit la Hierusalem et le Pastor Fido, c'est à dire les Chef-d'oeuvres des deux plus grands Poëtes de de-là les Monts; apres lesquels peu de gens auroient bonne grace de murmurer contre la Censure, et de s'offencer d'avoir *une aventure pareille à la leur*" (italics added).

Corneille, to whom this last remark was undoubtedly directed, hesitated for a while but eventually took Chapelain's advice to heart. He opted to look on the Quarrel, not as a persecution, but rather as a noble encounter, nobly engaged in, from which mutual benefits might be expected to come. The model for this type of encounter was, of course, the *duellum* such as Dante, for example, had described it in his *De Monarchia* (2. 9–13). In putting the concept of *duellum* at the very center of his next play, Corneille must surely have been thinking back to the Quarrel and to his own dilemma at its conclusion.

His first reaction upon reading the *Sentiments* had been to set to work preparing a reply. Boisrobert made it clear, however, that to do so would be to anger Richelieu. Corneille had to choose, then, between persisting in the defense of his play or abandoning it out of deference to the cardinal. Realism and prudence prevailed, but the playwright was not proud of himself:

> . . . Maintenant que vous me conseillez de n'y répondre point, veu les personnes qui s'en sont mêlées, il ne me faut point d'interprète pour entendre cela; je suis un peu plus de ce monde qu'Héliodore, qui aima mieux perdre son Evesché que son livre, et j'aime mieux les bonnes grâces de mon Maistre que toutes les réputations de la terre. (Gasté, p. 488)

Heliodorus's refusal to repudiate the work of his youth—the *Aethiopica*, which related the love and adventures of Theagenes and Chariclea—appealed to the imagination of the beleaguered playwright as a perfect example of resistance to pressure, an example that he himself obviously admired but could not or would not follow.

If one is to judge by the letter that Chapelain wrote to Balzac a year later, Corneille had a hard time coming to terms with himself about the outcome of the Quarrel: "Il ne fait plus rien, et Scudéry a du moins gagné cela, en le querellant, qu'il l'a rebuté du métier et lui a tari sa veine" (Mongrédien, p. 85). Instead of turning his attention to the future, he remained obsessed with the past: "Il ne parle plus que de règles et que de choses qu'il eût pu répondre aux Académiciens, s'il n'eût point craint de choquer les puissances." He had accepted his fate outwardly but not inwardly. He kept silent in public, only to complain endlessly in private. And his art was suffering.

If he had followed the example of Heliodorus or if he had remained forever divided against himself, Corneille might never have written another play. He most certainly would not have written *Horace*, for *Horace* not only articulates the main options open to Corneille at this juncture, it reflects the very dynamics of his choice among them. The play, I have said, assumes the allegory of the formal *duellum*, together with all the conditions and all the faith in Providence that go along with it. Of all the characters, only Horace gives himself up wholeheartedly to this enterprise, however; the others all hold back in some way or other. Though he has a wife and a father, Horace is perhaps closest to Curiace and Camille. During the course of the play, it is with them that he has his most painful confrontations, two instances of what the hero himself refers to as a "combat contre un autre soi-même." In real life Corneille appears to have begun by choosing acceptance over rebellion, then later on to have made a secondary choice between whole- and halfhearted commitment to the principle of acceptance. In the play this order is reversed, probably to enhance both the dramatic and the ethical effect. Horace confronts his weaker, more irresolute self first, in the scenes with Curiace in act 2; then, in the highly charged dramatic situation of act 4, he confronts the temptation to strong but negative commitment in his sister, Camille.

As he shaped the material borrowed from Roman history, Corneille infused it, then, with the urgency of his own dilemmas. The sympathy that he elicits for Curiace and Camille and the hint of brutishness with which he endows Horace suggest that, though he had taken the option represented by Horace, he still felt very close to the other two, rejected options also.

To be sure, *Horace* is not an allegory of the conventional

sort. But, along with its primary story of an early Roman hero, it seems to reenact the parallel story of the poet's own ordeal, his own encounter with destiny. On one level, then, Corneille literalizes Chapelain's allegory of the *duellum*; but on another, he develops it still further.

Polyeucte *and the Allegory of Iconoclasm.*

Respect for the other person is central in Corneille, as it is in the ideal of the *duellum.* Horace bears no hatred for Curiace or Camille, nor Polyeucte for Pauline or Félix. The magnificent exchange between Polyeucte and Pauline in act 4 constitutes a kind of *duellum*, greatly transposed but true to the inner spirit of the original model:

—Imaginations!
　　　　　—Célestes vérités!
—Etrange aveuglement!
　　　　　　—Eternelles clartés!
—Tu préfères la mort à l'amour de Pauline!
—Vous préférez le monde à la bonté divine!

(4. 3. 1285–88)

By the end of the play, Providence will have granted victory to Polyeucte, a victory in which, according to the promise, Pauline and Félix may also share. *Polyeucte* thus retains much of the ideology of *Horace*; but it adds something new of great importance, something centering on the violent act that Polyeucte performs in the pagan temple when he destroys the idol.

The Quarrel raised anew the age-old question of the relationship of art to truth. In *L'Illusion comique*, a few months before the *Cid*, Corneille had celebrated the power of the dramatic poet to create illusions; and the image, or allegory, that he employed to stand for the dramatist was that of a magician, Alcandre. Whether with this fact in mind or not, Corneille's critics during the Quarrel took great delight in making references to the "fausse gloire," the "faux esclat," the "fausses beautez" of the *Cid*; and in dubbing its author himself a mountebank, an alchemist, a worker of enchantments, and a magician. Mairet, dismissing a play of his own the better to attack Corneille, wrote that "la Silvie de Mairet, et le Cid de Corneille, ou de Guillen de Castro, comme il vous plairra sont les deux pieces de Theatre, dont les beautez apparentes, et phantastiques, ont le plus abusé d'honnestes gens" (Gasté, p. 286). The public's blindness was soon likened to idolatry, and it became the goal of Corneille's opponents to bring down the "idol" of the *Cid* and to convert the *Cid*'s "idolaters" to the truth. Faucon de Ris seems to have been the first to use the image, writing that, having seen the light himself, "je fis donc resolution de guerir ses idolatres de leur aveuglement" (Gasté, p. 203). Mairet, among others, picked up the figure of speech and developed it at length. Faucon de Ris had hailed the *Observations* of Scudéry for opening the eyes of the blind; Mairet, for his part, in his "Epistre familiere" to Corneille, credits Scudéry with having won still more converts with the proofs he had offered the Academy in substantiation of his charges against the *Cid*. Little by little the number of the deceived are diminishing, he says; and he looks forward to the day when the Academy will complete the process of conversion:

> Je vous asseure que vostre Cid a bien perdu de son embonpoint depuis quelque temps, et qu'on peut dire justement de luy,
>
> > *Qu'il est sur le Parnasse un Idole brisé,*
> > *Et que de jour en jour sa secte diminüe*
> > *Tant il est malayse*
> > *De ne pas embrasser la vérité connüe.*
> >
> > (Gasté, p. 288)

> . . . Vous estiez encore en possession de cette fausse gloire que le Cid vous a donnée; vous aviez encore le peuple et la pluspart des femmes de vostre costé; de facon que si vous eussiez eu seulement l'adresse de chicaner bien à propos il vous estoit facile d'empescher la conversion de ces Idolatres, qui se fussent bien contenté de l'apparence de vos raisons, puis qu'ils avoient pû s'esbloüyr au faux esclat de vostre Chef-d'oeuvre. (Gasté, p. 292)

> Il est indubitable que le champ de bataille vous demeuroit, mais apres que Monsieur de Scudery vous a convaincu luy-mesme de fausseté par une ample et autentique preuve des passages alleguez contre le Cid qu'il adresse à Messieurs de l'Academie, les plus raisonnables de vostre secte n'ont pas fait difficulté de l'abjurer ouvertement et les plus obstinez se sont contentez de dire qu'ils aymoient mieux mourir Heretiques, que d'estre sujets à la honte de confesser publiquement leur erreur. J'espere neantmoins que l'exemple des meilleurs es-

prits obligera bien-tost ces honnestes vergongneux à se ranger insensiblement au bon party, principalement apres ce qu'en doit prononcer l'Illustre Academie, au jugement de laquelle vous eussiez fait tres-sagement de vous soubmettre de bonne heure, et de bonne grace. (Gasté, pp. 293–94)

In the closing pages of the *Sentiments*, Chapelain alludes indirectly to this same leitmotiv of conversion to the truth. The Academy, he says, has labored selflessly for the good of all; and its fondest hope is to see "le plaisir d'une veritable connoissance" replace "celuy d'une douce illusion." Since the Academy seeks the instruction of the ignorant rather than glory for itself, it does not ask for any public display of recantation: "Il luy suffit qu'ils se condamnent en particulier, et qu'ils se rendent en secret à leur propre raison" (Gasté, p. 414). At the same time that he thus moderates the allegory of conversion, Chapelain modulates the concept of error and correction of error into the theory of rectification that we have been examining throughout this study. The *Cid*, he thought, had not been all false; and where it was false, it was only perpetuating errors inherited from the past. History, for Chapelain, brought with it a progressive revelation of truth. What Guillén de Castro or the Ancients mistook for truth cannot be adopted innocently by a poet living in France in the seventeenth century. The poet of today, full of respect as he is for the Ancients, must correct their errors:

. . . Les fautes mesmes des Anciens qui semblent devoir estre respectées pour leur vieillesse, ou si on l'ose dire, pour leur immortalité, ne peuvent pas defendre les siennes. Il est vray que celles la ne sont presque considerées qu'avec reverence, d'autant que les unes estant faittes devant les regles, sont nées libres et hors de leur jurisdiction, et que les autres par une longue durée ont comme acquis une prescription legitime. Mais cette faveur qui à peine met à couvert ces grands Hommes, ne passe point jusques à leurs successeurs. Ceux qui viennent apres eux heritent bien de leurs richesses, mais non pas de leurs privileges, et les vices d'Euripide ou de Seneque ne sçauroient faire approuver ceux de Guillen de Castro. . . . Le Pöete François qui nous a donné le Cid, est [donc] coupable de toutes les fautes qu'il n'y a pas corrigées. (Gasté, pp. 415–16)

The theory of rectification alerts the modern poet to the necessity for recasting those elements of a subject that time has revealed to be false; it thus protects him from the danger of raising up what for him and his age would be a false idol.

In choosing for the last play of the trilogy a Christian hero who is an iconoclast, Corneille appears again to have literalized one of the dominant allegories of the Quarrel. Polyeucte destroys the pagan idol during the temple ceremony as a means of demonstrating the new Christian truth that burns within him. This act of literal iconoclasm serves to sum up a whole series of other iconoclastic gestures that Corneille himself is making about poetry in and through the play. At the end of the trilogy, the playwright openly affirms the Christian ideology implicit in the preceding two pagan plays. He is thus destroying an illusion. At the same time, inasmuch as he rectifies book 4 of the *Aeneid* and, in the process, the *Cid*, he also refashions the partially false or defective images of Dido and Aeneas and of Chimène into more perfect, more truthful images. Finally, he takes Tasso's "erroneous" denial of perfection in any but the epic hero and, in its place, sets up as true the new image of a tragic hero without flaw.

Chapelain spoke of the "heureuse violence" by which "on tire la Verité du fons des abysmes." He was thinking of the violence of literary controversy allegorized as a kind of *duellum*, but he might just as well have said it in the context of the recasting of an icon. In order to make *Polyeucte*, Corneille had to do some violence to Vergil and to Tasso as well as to himself as author of the *Cid*; but he directed the violence not at individual poets or at individual poems but rather at the errors they happened to carry within them. Just as Polyeucte loves Pauline while hating her blindness, so Corneille respects the works that he chooses to rectify. Polyeucte would like to lead Pauline to God, and in the end he does. *Mutatis mutandis*, Corneille's goal in writing *Polyeucte* was to bring Dido and Chimène out of their error into the presence finally of Christ. A number of saints' stories might have served the playwright's purpose of rectifying the *Aeneid* and the *Cid*. Almost any Christian hero who could seem to abandon his wife might have satisfied the requirements. Polyeucte, however, was not only a Christian and a martyr and a husband who "left" his wife; he was also a destroyer of false images. As such he must have appeared to Corneille as, indeed, the perfect hero for the occasion.[1]

Théodore *and the Allegory of Persecution*

The Christians in *Polyeucte* suffer persecution, but the play concentrates more on the hero's provocation of his persecutor than on the evils of persecution itself. Persecution becomes the dominant theme in *Théodore*, however; and for Corneille it offers a third (and I think last) occasion for extending an allegory first encountered in the Quarrel. The Quarrel, I have said, was widely referred to as the "persecution" of the *Cid*. It is necessary, however, to divide the controversy into two phases: a preliminary, more or less personal phase during which individual writers and their supporters traded insults and accusations; then, with the intervention of the Academy, a second, formal, judicial phase consisting of more or less secret deliberations behind closed doors. Only the last phase qualifies as a possible persecution because only the Academy, backed by Richelieu, had any real power. Corneille no doubt felt harassed by the attacks of Mairet and Scudéry, but at least he was free then to counterattack. The Academy had been set up to foster the development of French letters, but from the outset Corneille opposed the idea of referring the debate to the Academy. He also opposed the idea of measuring the *Cid*, not by the standard of recent French plays, which he knew were inferior to his own, but rather by the ideal standard of the theorists and, in particular, the "Observateur." In the end he was forced to consent to procedures that he felt to be patently unjust. Since he was not a member of the Academy, he was not allowed to take any part at all in the deliberations. The fate of his play was to be decided in his absence and without his testimony being heard. During the five months that it took the Academy to weigh the evidence and reach its verdict, all Corneille could do was wait and meditate on the pitiful state of impotence to which he had been reduced: "J'attens avec beaucoup d'impatience les Sentimens de l'Académie, afin d'apprendre ce que doresenavant je dois suivre; jusques-là je ne puis travailler qu'avec défiance, et n'ose employer un mot en seureté" (Gasté, p. 485). If Corneille is being ironic here, as Jacques Maurens has suggested (p. 251), it is only because irony, like gallows humor, is one of the last defenses of the condemned. The author of the *Cid* was surely the first to believe in his own persecution.[2]

Placide's situation in act 4 of *Théodore* recapitulates the main aspects of Corneille's situation during the deliberations of the Academy. Placide loves Théodore, wishes to protect her, and will suffer a loss of honor himself should anything dishonorable happen to her. He is forced into inactivity, however, by means of a Machiavellian trick played on him by Marcelle. Marcelle promises to protect Théodore, then, with the gullible Placide lulled into false security, secretly orders Théodore taken to the brothel. Placide learns of his error too late and for most of act 4 is condemned to endure the torments of a protracted interval of waiting to find out what Théodore's fate has been. The concordance of Placide's suffering with Corneille's is striking; but, before we can speak of allegory, it is necessary to consider other parallels, too, parallels having to do with Théodore.

The judgment that the Academy finally handed down on Chimène was severe and went a very long way toward supporting the charges that Scudéry had made. Here is how the *Sentiments* ruled on the lovers' first interview, in act 3:

> L'Observateur apres cela passe à l'examen des moeurs attribuées à Chimène, et les condamne. En quoy nous sommes entierement de son costé; car au moins ne peut-on nier qu'elle ne soit, contre la bien seance de son sexe, Amante trop sensible, et Fille trop desnaturée. Quelque violence que luy peust faire sa passion, il est certain qu'elle ne devoit point se relascher dans la vengeance de la mort de son Pere, et moins encore se resoudre à espouser celuy qui l'avoit fait mourir. En cecy il faut avoüer que ses moeurs sont du moins scandaleuses, si en effect elles ne sont depravées. (Gasté, p. 372)

Chimène does not redeem herself in the Academy's eyes during the second interview, in act 5. On the contrary, "[elle] y abandonne tout ce qui luy restoit de pudeur" (Gasté, p. 389). This is precisely the kind of condemnation that Corneille had reason to fear when the Quarrel entered into its second phase, for during the initial phase his critics had already proved relentless in their attacks on Chimène.[3] Scudéry had set the tone in the *Observations* with a string of epithets ranging from "fille desnaturée," "cette Danaide," and "cette impudique" all on one page (Gasté, p. 80), to "ce Monstre" (p. 82), to "cette criminelle" (p. 93). He finally went so far as to liken her to a prostitute in act 5: "Elle luy dit cent choses dignes d'une prostituée, pour l'obliger à tuer ce pauvre sot de Don Sanche . . . " (p. 94). The threat of enforced prostitution that faces Théodore and, through Théodore, Placide as well thus parallels the fate that had befallen Chimène and Corneille during the second part of the Quarrel. During the long deliberations of the Academy, Corneille no doubt hoped that the Academy would clear his heroine's reputation, but he obviously knew that it might also do just the opposite. The ordeal in *Théodore* reflects the playwright's ordeal in the Quarrel down to the common specter of possible defilement.

Corneille had, of course, tried to counter the effect of Scudéry's accusation, first, by noting the favorable reaction of the court toward Chimène:

> Quand vous avez traicté la pauvre Chimene d'impudique, de prostituée, de parricide, de monstre; Ne vous estes vous pas souvenu, que la Reyne, les Princesses, et les plus vertueuses Dames de la Cour et de Paris, l'ont receuë et caressée en fille d'honneur . . . [?] (Gasté, p. 148)

and later on by pointing out how many recent heroines of the French stage were infinitely more deserving of Scudéry's epithets than poor Chimène. Of these, the most notorious seemed to him the gaily immoral heroine of Mairet's *Galanteries du duc d'Ossonne* (written in 1626 but published only in 1636):

> Je vous donneray seulement un mot d'advis avant que d'achever, [qui] est de ne mesler plus d'impietez dans les prostitutions de vos Heroines[;] les signes de Croix de vostre Flavie [= les signes de croix qu'elle fait ironiquement juste avant de pécher] et les Anges de lumiere de vostre Duc [= les anges qu'il invoque par moquerie], sont des profanations qui font horreur à tout le monde. (Gasté, p. 327)

It can scarcely be an accident that Marcelle's sickly daughter, whose hopeless love for Placide sets the persecution in motion, also bears the name Flavie. Corneille, it would seem, wants the opposition Théodore/Flavie, among other things, to figure the opposition Chimène/Flavie that developed in the course of the Quarrel in connection with the attempted vilification of Chimène.

At the very start of the Quarrel, still another opposition had developed—between the muses of Corneille and Mairet. Corneille's muse, briefly glimpsed in the closing lines of the "Excuse," is presented as free and capricious—free, because she insists on satisfying herself rather than others, including the supposedly influential Ariste, who has requested a song; capricious, no doubt because capriciousness in a young woman is an acceptable way of accounting for intransigence:

> N'y penses plus, Ariste, une telle injustice
> Exposeroit ma Muse à son plus grand supplice,
> Laissez la tousjours libre agir suivant son choix
> Ceder à son caprice et s'en faire des loix.
>
> (Gasté, p. 66)

In Corneille's view the muse of his rival Mairet was totally different. In the "Excuse" he had expressed great scorn for the poet who lowers himself to making the rounds "de Reduit en Reduit" in search of supporters for his work. Stung by the "Excuse," Mairet had replied with a poem denouncing Corneille for his overweening pride and accusing him of having plagiarized Guillén de Castro:

> Je croy que ce suject esclatant sur la Scene,
> Puis qu'il ravit le Tage a pu ravir la Seine.
> Mais il ne falloit pas en offencer l'*Autheur*,
> Et par une impudence en orgueil confirmée,
> Asseurer d'un langage aussi vain qu'imposteur,
> Que tu dois à toy seul toute ta Renommée.
>
> (Gasté, p. 67)

Corneille replied to this reply with a violent direct attack on Mairet and Mairet's muse:

> Chacun connoist son jaloux naturel
> Le monstre au doigt comme un fou solennel,
> Et ne croit pas, en sa bonne escriture,
>   Qu'il face mieux [.]
> Paris entier ayant leu son cartel,
> L'envoye au Diable, et sa Muse au Bordel.
>
> (Gasté, p. 70)

The "Advertissement au Besançonnois Mairet," at the same time it formulates the opposition Chimène/Flavie, reiterates the opposition of a pure Cornelian muse, on the one hand, and a corrupt, infinitely compromised Mairetian muse, on the other: "On sçait le petit commerce que vous pratiquez, et que vous n'avez point d'applaudissemens que vous ne gaigniez à force de Sonnets et de reverences. Si vous envoyiez vos pieces de Besançon, comme Mr Corneille envoye les siennes de Roüen, sans interesser personne en leur succez, vous tomberiez bien bas . . . " (Gasté, pp. 324–25).

Théodore first appears in act 2. She has been summoned to the palace in circumstances that do not bode well. As she is waiting to see Valens and Marcelle, she talks with her cousin-confidant Cléobule. For safety's sake, Cléobule presses her to relent and choose a husband: "Dans un péril si grand faites un protecteur" (l. 421). The scene is clearly a variation of the traditional opening scene in a pastoral, wherein a friend urges the chaste heroine to taste of the fruits of love. Here, it is not just the heroine's happiness but her very life that is at stake. Théodore remains adamant and refuses all prospect of marriage, however. For the time being, she does not wish to divulge her specific reason (which is that she has already promised herself to God), but she offers Cléobule a choice of three general motives for refusal, any one of which, she implies, would be sufficient:

> Voilà quelle je suis et quelle je veux être;
> La raison quelque jour s'en fera mieux connoître:
> Nommez-la cependant vertu, caprice, orgueil,
> Ce dessin me suivra jusque dans le cercueil.
>
> (2. 2. 407–10)

Théodore has all the attributes originally associated with the Cornelian muse. Fiercely independent, she will accept help from her protectors if necessary (at least from Didyme), but whether out of virtue, capriciousness, or pride, she will never consent to enter into a marriage with them.

Between Placide and Théodore, Corneille has succeeded, then, in evoking the ordeal of the poet (reduced to impotence), the ordeal of the heroine (threatened with defilement), and the virginal purity of the poet's muse, as the Quarrel had variously revealed them. He does not seem to be allegorizing because as usual he has taken care to literalize, on one level, all the allegories that he has taken over from the past. There can be little doubt, however, that he intended us to read *Théodore* on more than its literal level.

The renewal of interest that Corneille shows in the Quarrel at this relatively late date poses something of a problem, however. One can easily understand why the controversy should have been uppermost in his mind when he was writing *Horace* and *Polyeucte*; he was struggling to prove himself, struggling to transcend the limitations of the *Cid* and, if possible, win acclaim eventually as the new Tasso. Between *Polyeucte* and *Théodore*, however, there lies a considerable interval—four years and as many plays—during which time he evinced no discernible interest in returning to the allegorical frame of reference of the Quarrel. Something must have happened to stir up memories of earlier days. In fact, I think it was a combination of several factors. For one thing, the source material he was using probably acted to stimulate him to think allegorically about poetry and the poet. Godeau, in a narrative poem on the subject, "La Vierge d'Antioche," as well as in the "Discours" that served as a preface to his *Oeuvres chrestiennes* (1641), had interpreted Theodora's story as an allegory of the redemption of poetry through the sacrifice of martyrs' blood; that is, as a rectification of poetry itself insofar as poetry dedicated itself to Christian truths.[4] Corneille's heroine figures the Cornelian muse more than she seems to figure anything like the Christian muse, but the playwright may well have begun with the broader allegory and little by little particularized it as he was working with the subject. The *Aminta*, on the other hand, offered him, at the end of act 1, a charming little allegory of the happy results of enlightened patronage. Corneille had only to reverse the terms of patronage—and the tragic genre in which he had elected to work would naturally have favored such a reversal—in order to go from the idyllic to the horrific, from ideal protection of the poet to his outright persecution.

Corneille seems to have written *Théodore* sometime during the course of 1644, when his enthusiasm for Mazarin knew no bounds. The cardinal had immensely gratified the playwright the year before by granting him a pension even before the playwright had had time to petition him for one. Corneille had expressed his gratitude twice already, first, with a poem of "Remerciement," then with the dedication of *Pompée* to his new patron in February of 1644. *Théodore*, I suspect, was to have been another, more elaborate celebration of Mazarin's qualities as a patron. Mazarin's ties with the Barberini family in Rome were common knowledge. This family—notably the cardinals Antonio and Francesco and their uncle, the pope Urban VIII—had protected Mazarin before Mazarin came to France. They had also protected dramatic poetry: the Barberini palace had its own sumptuous theater, and it was there, during two consecutive carnival seasons, that the *Teodora* of Rospigliosi had been performed to great acclaim. Through a French *Théodore*, Corneille could draw attention to the Roman origins of the enlightened patronage that Mazarin had just introduced into France. If the play had not failed, my guess is that the author would have dedicated the work to the cardinal, in a letter referring to the earlier Barberini *Teodora*.[5]

Of course, Corneille could have written a new version of the Theodora story without connecting it to the allegory of the Quarrel. And it is not readily apparent, perhaps, how insistence on the theme of persecution together with allegorical reference to the Quarrel could serve the playwright's supposed purpose of hailing Mazarin as a model patron. One must remember, however, that freedom to complain is a precious right not enjoyed by victims of repression. Public complaint about persecution, especially past persecution, is often a sure sign that persecution has been lifted. Corneille had agreed, reluctantly, not to publish an answer to the *Sentiments*; and in the Epître for *Horace*, he had done more than make his peace with Richelieu. He had opted to put all thoughts of persecution behind him and to concentrate on moving forward, dialectically, from his position in the *Cid*. The death of Richelieu, followed by the advent of Mazarin, in all probability resulted in the playwright's experiencing a sudden sense of relaxation. Under Mazarin he was free to look back in a way that he could not have afforded to do earlier. In this psychological context, it is not hard to see how his sources might have prompted him to go back to the Quarrel and to give expression now to long-repressed thoughts and emotions. Corneille was perhaps not altogether proud of his own conduct following the Quarrel. He probably had a bad conscience about yielding to force (his admiration for Heliodorus would suggest as much). And he probably wrote the Epître for *Horace* in partially bad faith, attributing a very great deal more influence to Richelieu than actually existed. If all this be so, then Corneille may even have looked on *Théodore* as a kind of rectification of past errors, a means of setting the record straight now that he was free to tell the truth. Strange as it seems at first, the negativities of *Théodore* could very well have been intended after all as an expression of real affirmation.

Allegorizing in literary debate did not begin with the Quarrel of the *Cid*. As Marc Fumaroli has shown, it was a vigorous phenomenon in France during the period 1578–1630, when its principal focus was prose ("Rhétorique, dramaturgie, critique littéraire"). During the 1630s, as theoretical interest shifted from prose to dramatic poetry, literary debate and its attendant allegories spilled over into the theater, with plays like *L'Illusion comique, Les Visionnaires,* and *La Comédie des Académistes.* The allegorizing that has concerned us here is something new, however, or at least different. For in *Horace, Polyeucte,* and *Théodore,* Corneille is writing tragedy, a genre whose aims far transcend the limited frame of reference of literary debate. He wants, in these works, not to inform or persuade his audience but to stir, if he can, their very deepest emotions. Ultimately, however, he wants also to assure himself great fame as a poet, as great a fame as Tasso had won, or Homer and Vergil before him. It is this personal quest that sometimes reveals itself allegorically in Corneille's tragic theater. The Quarrel of the *Cid* contributed more than anything else to the definition of the playwright's quest, and, that being so, it is not surprising that the allegories through which he later chose to express his authorial aims, interests, or anxieties should also have come from the Quarrel.

PART II: THE "DISCOURS DE LA TRAGÉDIE"

In the preface to his translation of the *Imitation de Jésus-Christ* (1656), Corneille indicated that he was already at work on the collected edition of his plays that would appear four years later. He refers to the Examens, though not by that name: fresh commentaries on each individual play to replace the prefaces that had been accumulating regularly all along. They would be, he says, "[des] réflexions sur chaque poëme, tirées de l'art poétique." Among other things, he hoped they would serve as a guide for "ceux qui se voudront exercer en ce genre de poésie" (*Oeuvres* 8:12 n. 8). He did not, in 1656, mention the three discourses. Who conceived the idea of having one discourse for each of the three volumes of the collected works we do not know. It was likely Corneille himself, though it may also have been his publisher. In any event, the discourses were destined to fulfill an important function over and above any considerations of textual layout. The poetics on which Corneille said he was going to base the individual reflections (that is, the Examens) did not exist in 1656—or existed only in scattered, incomplete statements and in the playwright's own head. For Aristotle's *Poetics* would obviously not do, at least not without substantial revision. The *Discours* supplied what was missing, a formal Cornelian poetics to which the Examens could refer.

Corneille throughout his career had demonstrated considerable independence of mind as regards Aristotle. At the outset he had adopted the attitude that the "rules" were no more than an interesting option, which a playwright could exercise or not as he wished. In the dedicatory letter for *La Suivante*, which came out while the Academy was deliberating the fate of the *Cid*, Corneille had already begun to moderate his stand, however, and expressed a willingness, in the interest of attaining "un applaudissement universel," to take steps to please the learned critics in his audience as well as the general public. That he acted on these intentions is proved by the greater care he took, beginning with *Horace*, to incorporate Aristotelian principles into his now tighter dramaturgy. It is only in the preface to *Polyeucte* (the "Abrégé du Martyre de saint Polyeucte"), however, that he began, tentatively, to comment critically on his efforts to "regularize" his theater.

By 1648, when he wrote the Avertissement for the *Cid*, to appear in a collected edition published that same year, his attitude toward Aristotle had matured; and he was able to articulate very clearly what, in his mind, had to be adhered to in the *Poetics* and what could, and should, be revised:

> Ce grand homme [Aristote] a traité la poétique avec tant d'adresse et de jugement, que les préceptes qu'il nous en a donnés sont de tous les temps et de tous les peuples; et bien loin de s'amuser au travail des bienséances et des agréments, qui peuvent être divers selon que ces deux circonstances sont diverses, il a été droit aux mouvements de l'âme, dont la nature ne change point. Il a montré quelles passions la tragédie doit exciter dans celles de ses auditeurs; il a cherché quelles conditions sont nécessaires, et aux personnes qu'on introduit, et aux événements qu'on représente, pour les y faire naître; il en

> a laissé des moyens qui auroient produit leur effet partout dès la création du monde, et qui seront capables de le produire encore partout, tant qu'il y aura des théâtres et des auteurs; et pour le reste, que les lieux et les temps peuvent changer, il l'a négligé, et n'a pas même prescrit le nombre des actes, qui n'a été réglé que par Horace beaucoup après lui. (*Oeuvres,* 3:85–86)

Corneille stresses here more strongly than ever before his faith in the eternal verity of Aristotle's views concerning human nature and the dramatic poet's interest in appealing, through his art, to the deeper recesses of the heart. This ringing endorsement gives way in the end, however, to the equally important proviso that "pour le reste" there is nothing wrong with adding to the *Poetics.* To be sure, he does not venture to say that Aristotle is ever at fault and that succeeding generations, in what they have added, in effect have rectified the *Poetics.* Still, the view he defines here is clearly in harmony with the principle of rectification as we have seen it applied to poetry, and close to Tasso's idea of the constancy of poetic genres and poetic talent versus the evolution, through the ages, of heroic decorum. Corneille hints, in his remark about Horace and the convention of dividing plays into five acts, that criticism, like poetry itself, undergoes change as it moves from place to place and age to age. The *Discorsi* had sketched out a grand evolution in heroic decorum going from Homer's *Iliad* to Vergil's *Aeneid* down to modern Christian epic. Corneille seems to be assuming a like evolution in criticism— one that would run from Aristotle's *Poetics* to Horace's *Art of Poetry* to Tasso's *Discorsi* and, thence, by implication to his own critical view. That view achieved its full maturity only in the *Discours* of 1660, which besides echoing the *Discorsi* in its title also reflects a thoroughgoing modernism that the example of Tasso no doubt strengthened in the French poet.

The first and third discourses, on dramatic poetry and on the unities, offer the widest and the narrowest focuses on the playwright's art. The middle discourse, on tragedy, for many reasons claims priority of attention. Like books 2 and 3 of the *Discorsi,* it represents the essence of the author's thinking on poetics and contains his most vigorous and most original arguments. In what follows I shall therefore concentrate on the "Discours de la tragédie." The discourse is not easy to read because Corneille

adopts a strategy that does much to conceal the far-reaching implications of what he has to say. Instead of developing his own
ideas directly, as Tasso does in the *Discorsi*, Corneille most often
begins with Aristotle, whose ideas he is at pains to explicate as
thoroughly as possible before moving on to outline his own
theories, which he presents as extensions of, or options to, the
Poetics. Corneille obviously disagrees with Aristotle, or questions Aristotle's conclusions, on quite a few issues, but it is hard
to see on first or second reading exactly what the significance of
these divergencies is. For Corneille makes no attempt to separate the incidental from the essential or to connect one essential
point of difference with another. In the following analysis, I shall
try to do what the playwright chose not to do, in order to bring
out as forcefully as possible the real originality of his conception
of heroic tragedy.[6]

As in the Avertissement for the *Cid*, so in the discourses,
Corneille takes care to distinguish between what is eternally
valid in the *Poetics* and what is time- or culture-bound. For all his
professions of respect, one often gets the impression, nevertheless, that in Corneille's opinion Aristotle made more sense for
the Greeks than he does for Frenchmen living in the seventeenth
century. The playwright notes that the tragic emotions of pity and
fear are inspired, according to Aristotle, by the fate that befalls a
flawed hero, and the action of the tragedy is supposed somehow
to effect the purging of these same emotions. He expresses
doubt as to whether catharsis actually takes place in tragedy and
even hazards the opinion that Aristotle himself proposed the
theory only in order to combat Plato, who had condemned poets
and poetry as harmful to the republic. Aristotle's insistence that
the tragic hero must have a flaw, the playwright traces to another
accidental circumstance. The heroes of Greek tragedy, he points
out, were usually monarchs. The Greeks themselves, however,
cherished democratic ideals and so naturally delighted in seeing
kings and queens depicted as imperfect. The Greek tragedians,
he suggests, were only appealing to this anti-monarchical bias
when they created the model of the necessarily flawed tragic
hero.

Having thus characterized the *Poetics'* view of tragedy as
"Greek," Corneille proceeds to elaborate a series of alternatives.
A playwright may, but does not have to, follow the Greeks in

exciting pity and fear through the same hero. If he wishes, he may excite pity through one character and fear through another (as in *Rodogune*) or even choose to ignore fear altogether and excite only pity (as in *Polyeucte*). (In a passage later deleted, he considered the possibility that tragedy might also excite only fear, but rejected the idea on grounds that such a play would not work and that, furthermore, no example of the type appeared to exist.) The hero of these alternate forms of tragedy no longer need be flawed (e.g., Antiochus, Héraclius, and Nicomède) and indeed may be saintly (e.g., Polyeucte). And, in lieu of purgation, tragedies may now derive their usefulness either from "la naïve peinture des vices et des vertus" or from poetic justice.

The distance that Corneille places between his own theater and the Greeks' can best be measured, however, by seeing how he revises Aristotle's list of possible tragic situations. Aristotle observes, and Corneille agrees, that conflicts occurring between persons who are closely related to one another are the most apt to excite the tragic emotions. These persons may recognize one another or not, and the terrible acts that they are planning may or may not actually be performed. These factors give rise to four basic situations, which Aristotle ranks in order of their decreasing effectiveness as follows: (1) the act is planned in ignorance of a true relationship, then the true relationship is discovered and the act is not performed (as in *Iphigenia in Tauris*); (2) the act is performed in ignorance, after which the true relationship is discovered (as in *Oedipus*); (3) the act is planned and performed in full knowledge of the true relationship (as in *Medea*); and (4) the act is planned in full knowledge of the true relationship but then not performed (as in *Antigone*). Aristotle finds *Oedipus* more effective than *Medea* because the revelation of truth in *Oedipus* creates an agreeable surprise and, contrariwise, Medea's act, performed in full knowledge of her relationship to her children, provokes a sense of outrage. The fourth possibility he virtually rejects because this situation, he says, "merely shocks us, and, since no suffering is involved, it is not tragic. Hence nobody is allowed to behave like this, or only seldom, as when Haemon fails to kill Creon in the *Antigone*" (*Poetics* 14). Corneille's preferences are almost the reverse of Aristotle's. Situation (1)—in which an act is planned in ignorance, but not performed because of timely discovery of a true relationship—this situation, the playwright says, is capable of creating suspense but will not excite pity or elicit many tears. Furthermore, situations of this type must necessarily be invented by the poet, inasmuch as so few examples can be found in history, either because they have occurred only very infrequently or else because they have not been deemed worthy of being written about. Situation (2), as typified by *Oedipus*, stands to produce more interesting theatrical effects, he believes, but situations of this type are extremely rare. It is not often that closely related persons fail to recognize one another. The poet, moreover, cannot invent a situation of this sort; for the sake of credibility he is forced to use one of the few such situations provided by history or legend. Situation (3), which is represented by *Medea*, appeals to Corneille more than either of the other two. Though it too requires the support of history, it avoids the extreme of rarity found in (2), where violence occurs among closely related persons who do not recognize their relationship, but it does not fall into the domain of the commonplace, as in (1). Corneille's favorite situation, however, is the one that Aristotle had judged to be unsuitable: that in which the act is planned in full knowledge of a true relationship, but, for some reason or other, is not performed. This is the situation found not only in *Antigone* but also in *Le Cid, Cinna, Rodogune, Héraclius,* and *Nicomède*, he says. He agrees that the characters' failure to carry through with a planned course of action would be ineffective if it depended solely on an unmotivated change of heart; but, handled well, this situation seems to him to hold the greatest of possibilities:

> . . . Quand ils y font de leur côté tout ce qu'ils peuvent, et qu'ils sont empêchés d'en venir à l'effet par quelque puissance supérieure, ou par quelque changement de fortune qui les fait périr eux-mêmes, ou les réduit sous le pouvoir de ceux qu'ils vouloient perdre, il est hors de doute que cela fait une tragédie d'un genre peut-être plus sublime que les trois qu'Aristote avoue; et que s'il n'en a point parlé, c'est qu'il n'en voyoit point d'exemples sur les théâtres de son temps, où ce n'étoit pas la mode de sauver les bons par la perte des méchants. . . . (*Oeuvres*, 1:68–69)

The playwright tries to minimize the importance of his break with Aristotle by continuing to express the greatest respect for his predecessor, but his modernist position remains clear:

"Ce n'est pas démentir Aristote que de l'expliquer ainsi favo-rablement, pour trouver dans cette quatrième manière d'agir qu'il rebute, une espèce de nouvelle tragédie plus belle que les trois qu'il recommande, et qu'il leur eût sans doute préférée, s'il l'eût connue. C'est faire honneur à notre siècle, sans rien re-trancher à l'autorité de ce philosophe . . . " (*Oeuvres*, 1:69). Again, near the close of this section of the "Discours de la tra-gédie," the author sums up his thinking in the following paragraph:

> Il y a grande apparence que ce qu'a dit ce philosophe de ces divers degrés de perfection pour la tragédie avoit une entière justesse de son temps, et devant ses compatriotes; je n'en veux point douter; mais aussi je ne me puis empêcher de dire que le goût de notre siècle n'est point celui du sien sur cette pré-férence d'une espèce à l'autre, ou du moins que ce qui plaisoit au dernier point à ses Athéniens ne plaît pas également à nos François; et je ne sais point d'autre moyen de trouver mes doutes supportables, et demeurer tout ensemble dans la vé-nération que nous devons à tout ce qu'il a écrit de la poétique. (*Oeuvres*, 1:72)

Corneille's ideal hero is very good, then, if not perfect; and he naturally elicits the sympathy of the audience. ("[Cette] ma-xime de faire aimer nos principaux acteurs n'étoit pas de l'usage de nos anciens" [*Oeuvres*, 1:80]). Opposite him is a very wicked person who tries to achieve the hero's downfall. Aristotle thought that if either the very innocent or the very wicked were shown falling into misfortune, the audience would fail to expe-rience the proper tragic emotions. In one case, they would feel indignation toward the source of the misfortune rather than pity for the innocent hero. In the other case, they would experience neither pity (because the misfortune of the wicked character would be deserved) nor fear (because they could not identify with excessive wickedness). Corneille, on the contrary, claims that pity is not necessarily outweighed by indignation and that audiences can find something (of a lesser degree) with which to relate even in the most wicked. Consequently: "En voici deux ou trois manières [d'exposer sur la scène des hommes ou très ver-tueux ou très méchants qui sont dans le malheur], que peut-être Aristote n'a su prévoir, parce qu'on n'en voyoit pas d'exemples sur les théâtres de son temps" (*Oeuvres*, 1:63). Poetic justice is, in fact, a magnificent adornment. Combined with the audience's natural affection for innocence, it can produce a powerful effect in the theater: "Il semble alors que la justice du ciel ait présidé au succès, qui trouve d'ailleurs une croyance d'autant plus facile qu'il répond aux souhaits de l'auditoire, qui s'intéresse toujours pour ceux dont le procédé est le meilleur" (*Oeuvres*, 1:92). Poetic justice proves not only pleasing but morally useful as well: "Le fruit qui peut naître des impressions que fait la force de l'exemple lui manquoit [à Aristote] : la punition des méchantes actions, et la récompense des bonnes, n'étoient pas de l'usage de son siècle . . . " (*Oeuvres*, 1:58).

Corneille never tries to specify in detail what exactly determines the differences in usage or taste between ancient Greece and modern France. He speaks, but only in passing, of the denouement that seems to imply "la justice du ciel" (*Oeuvres*, 1:92 and 79). Elsewhere he notes that "il faut s'accommoder aux moeurs de l'auditeur et à plus forte raison à sa croyance"; Christians, he says, will not tolerate the intervention of Greek gods into the action of a modern play, "parce que nous en savons manifestement la fausseté, et que [ces apparitions] choquent notre religion" (*Oeuvres*, 1:75–76). Undoubtedly it is Christianity that makes the difference throughout, but Corneille does not emphasize the fact, as Tasso does in the *Discorsi*. He is constrained probably by the unresolved conflict in the society around him between the belief that the theater can and should aim at the utmost seriousness and the contrary belief that the theater, even though purified, is still unworthy of dealing with the most serious subject of all, the Christian faith. Corneille points a very tentative finger toward this contradiction later on in the paragraph just quoted from. Apollo and Mercury, he says, would prove displeasing in a modern play. Playwrights can always make adjustments, and a Christian playwright in theory might be expected to substitute angels and saints for the gods of the Ancients. Such is not the case, however: "Qu'auroit-on dit, si pour démêler Héraclius d'avec Martian, après la mort de Phocas, je me fusse servi d'un ange? Ce poëme est entre des chrétiens, et cette apparition y auroit eu autant de justesse que celles des Dieux de l'antiquité dans ceux des Grecs; c'eût été néanmoins un secret infaillible de rendre celui-là ridicule . . . " (*Oeuvres*, 1:76). Corneille approaches the problem in typically indirect fashion by focusing on the device of the deus ex machina, where the ancillary problem of arbitrariness tends to confuse the basic issue of the acceptability of direct divine intervention in the theater. The conventions of the modern epic allowed for free and open interaction of the divine and the human planes; neither Tasso nor any of his French imitators needed skirt the issue either in their poems or in their theoretical works. Corneille, as we saw, had to replace the god Mercury with a human agent, Néarque, in *Polyeucte*; and in the "Discours de la tragédie," he permits himself only the most oblique reference to the real nature of the gulf dividing his theater from the Greeks'.

In the last half of the "Discours de la tragédie," Corneille moves on to another, related problem. Ostensibly he is scrutinizing each of Aristotle's four basic situations to see for which ones the poet must turn to history or legend and to what extent the poet is free to modify what he borrows. Indirectly, Corneille is discussing rather how to adjust any material, whether borrowed from history or from the work of an ancient poet, so as to make it conform to his own preferred range of tragic possibilities. Corneille has no interest in a play that is totally invented by the poet. The central incident must be extraordinary and therefore requires the support of some known or citable precedent. Aristotle's first choice among the four situations, it will be recalled, seemed quite uninteresting to Corneille precisely because it involved commonplace happenings: the planning of action in ignorance, followed by cancellation of the plan after discovery of a truth. Here, Corneille thinks that the poet not only might but would probably have to invent, since history books rarely report such mundane affairs. Clearly, what interests Corneille must come from history or legend; but it has to be adapted to a special mold.

He cites Antiochus and Nicomède as examples of historical figures whom he changed for the better. The first, having become suspicious of his mother, in historical fact forced her to drink poison. Corneille retains the death by poisoning of Cléopâtre but does not make Antiochus the cause of that death. As a consequence, he says, Cléopâtre's punishment appears even more exemplary than it does in history; moreover, the punishment is brought about with no loss of audience sympathy for Antiochus. Similarly, Corneille's Nicomède has the power to cause his father's death, but unlike the historical Nicomède, he does not do so. Corneille does not admit to rewriting the works of ancient poets along the same lines, but it is clear he did precisely that in both *Polyeucte* and *Rodogune* itself. What he does do, as we have seen elsewhere, is to theorize about a possible rectification of Sophocles' *Electra*: "Pour rectifier ce sujet à notre mode, il faudroit qu'Oreste n'eût dessein que contre Egisthe; qu'un reste de tendresse respectueuse pour sa mère lui en fît remettre la punition aux Dieux; que cette reine s'opiniâtrât à la protection de son adultère, et qu'elle se mît entre son fils et lui si malheureusement qu'elle reçût le coup que ce prince voudroit porter à cet assassin de son père" (*Oeuvres*, 1:81).

Weaving a circuitous path through questions of the necessary and the verisimilar, on the one hand, and of regular and extraordinary verisimilitude on the other, Corneille defines his own idea of a theater with intermittent clarity. The poet may, if he wants, invent everything or nothing, imagine all the characters and all the action or merely dramatize history. Whichever path he chooses, he will not be violating the rules of his art. To test himself to the utmost, however, to attain the highest reaches of the playwright's art, he must take the risk of mixing fact and fiction (*Oeuvres*, 1:83). For it is through verisimilitude that the dramatic poet works his greatest effects, and particularly through "la vraisemblance extraordinaire." Corneille never rejects outright anything found in the *Poetics*; but he is forever modifying, attenuating, accommodating, or simply adding to what Aristotle has said. He is, in short, rectifying Aristotle without saying so outright.

In his letter to the Abbé de Pure (*Oeuvres*, 10:485–87), Corneille indicated that writing the three discourses had not come easily; and in truth the strain shows. The problem was that he was trying to reconcile too many disparate ideas and please too many factions while still remaining true to his new vision of tragedy. Certain of the great prefaces provide, on isolated topics, a stronger sense of the playwright's originality as a theoretician: the preface to *La Suite du Menteur* on the question of utility; the prefaces of *Rodogune* and *Héraclius* on uses of history and invention; and the preface of *Nicomède* on the new hero without a tragic flaw. One would expect the "Discours de la tragédie" to pick up from this last preface the theory of the hero who excites neither pity nor fear but only *admiration.* No such thing occurs, however. *Admiration* is nowhere mentioned as an alternative tragic emotion; and, in contradiction to the preface of *Nicomède* (and also the Examen, which in this matter repeats the preface), the discourse looks on Nicomède only as a hero who excites pity: "L'auditeur peut avoir de la commisération pour Antiochus, pour Nicomède, pour Héraclius . . . " (*Oeuvres,* 1:60). The preface of *Nicomède* marks the farthest point that Corneille reaches in defining his new hero in terms normally associated not with tragedy but rather with the epic; and he retreats from that position, presumably out of respect for the *Poetics,* or out of fear of provoking his neo-Aristotelian critics.

The presence of Aristotle dominates the "Discours de la tragédie," distorting and inhibiting not so much Corneille's thought as his expression of it on the page. Tasso, in many ways, is just as powerful an influence as Aristotle. The Cornelian conception of a new tragic action owes a great deal to the *Discorsi,* even though Tasso would not have approved of the shift that Corneille makes from epic to tragedy. Tasso no doubt also contributed to the modernism that marks the "Discours de la tragédie," even though, because of the situation in France, Corneille feels obliged to mute it. His new tragic hero is always at least implicitly Christian; and the reshaping of history to accommodate this new model of heroic action is a form of Christian revisionism. If Corneille appeals insistently to Aristotle in the discourses, he does so with a clear sense of the great distance that separates them, of things that Aristotle did not see and could now know in his day—in short, of the new dispensation under which he himself, like Tasso, writes. Corneille would undoubtedly have disagreed with Aristotle in any event; but the example of Tasso very likely helped him define his independence.

As theoretical works the *Discorsi* and the *Discours* share many of the same aims.[7] Though Tasso almost never refers to his own work whereas Corneille always does, both are attempting to explain and to justify their own poetic practice and to situate it in the great poetic tradition inherited from the past, while demonstrating its relevance to the needs and the beliefs of the present. The greatest poets do not always let us see them reflecting as critics on the art they practice so well. Tasso and Corneille in this respect are quite exceptional, and their critical work is especially valuable for being conceived from within the citadel of poetic creativity. In writing the "Discours," Corneille thus went beyond the challenge laid down to him during the Quarrel of the *Cid*. He joined the twin traditions of greatness in poetry and greatness in poetic theory. Like Tasso, who had led the way and set the example, he distinguished himself finally not only as a poet but also as a critic of poetry.

The "Discours de la tragédie" is one kind of reflection on poetry; the literalization of critical metaphors that we saw in *Horace*, *Polyeucte*, and *Théodore* is another form of the same self-reflectiveness. What they show, taken together, is that throughout this crucial middle period of his long career, Corneille held fast to a single strong vision that he had forged from the double fires of the Quarrel of the *Cid* and his subsequent ardent desire to emulate Tasso. In this vision Corneille saw himself as a modern; that is, as a Christian poet, and his art as a modern, Christian art, however discreet he had to be about proclaiming it.

Conclusion

A NEW POETIC DISPENSATION BORN OF THE QUARREL OF the *Cid* governs the next seven of Corneille's heroic plays. As a vision of man and art, it retains the nobility of spirit that had marked the *Cid*, but adds a broader historical perspective and a much higher degree of literary self-consciousness. It implies a sense of high-serious adventure gravely undertaken as a supreme test of the validity both of the world and of the self. Emulation and rectification lie at the heart of the new vision. The poet, like his heroes, dares to measure himself by the highest standards there are, then aspires to become a standard of measurement himself. The plays embody the central vision with varying degrees of success. The vision itself remains in place at least as long as it takes the playwright to explore it fully from all angles.

The seven plays in question fall into two groups, separated by the comedies *Le Menteur* and *La Suite du Menteur*. The playwright's interests and modes of operation are substantially different in the two groups but are clearly relatable dialectically. The first group consists of the Roman plays: the trilogy and *La Mort de Pompée*. Corneille here borrows very heavily from the epic tradition. The ancient texts from which he was working and which he was intent on rectifying were the two best known Latin epics: the *Aeneid* for the trilogy and the *Pharsalia* for *Pompée*. The *De Monarchia* of Dante, an epic poet, appears to have suggested the Christian providential interpretation of Roman history that infuses the trilogy; and it is the modern Christian epic, as practiced by Tasso, that opens up a new, hopeful interlude in the otherwise closed historical framework of *Pompée*. In the second group of plays, Corneille chooses three dramatic texts to rectify, one from the ancient world (*Electra* in *Rodogune*) and two from the Cinquecento (Tasso's *Aminta* and *Torrismondo* respectively in *Théodore* and *Héraclius*). It is obvious that Corneille did not choose the subjects of these two groups of plays at random. The pattern of his choices clearly indicates that he wanted to exploit both types of heroic poetic texts, epic and dramatic, and wanted also to draw on the modern as well as the ancient literary legacy. Except perhaps for the *Pharsalia* and *Torrismondo*, the quality of the texts he chooses to correct is undeniable. He uses lesser texts along the way—the *Polietto* of Bartolommei, the *Teodora* of Rospigliosi, for example—but these are of secondary importance. They simply offer a means of transposing the much greater texts that the playwright is really working on.

Corneille had practiced rectification on a very limited scale before *Horace*: specifically in the little tragedy of act 5 of *L'Illusion comique*, which recasts some of the material of *Médée* in a more modern, more ethically acceptable form. He had also begun to think in terms of emulation in the dedicatory letter for *La Suivante*, but the poets he spoke of vying with and perhaps learning from were not the greatest poets of all time but his own French contemporaries. Corneille already knew a great deal about dramatic techniques and had the extraordinary dramatic imagination that was never to desert him; but before writing the trilogy, he had not yet placed himself, in his mind's eye, on the world stage of poetry. From the way he transposes events and images from the Quarrel into certain of his later plays, it is clear that he experienced the Quarrel of the *Cid* as a real trauma. By dint of his own heroic resolve, however, he turned it into something glorious; and as a consequence he emerged from the controversy with a heightened sense of his own potential as a poet, a deeper understanding of the history of poetry, and a much nobler sense of purpose.

The Quarrel of the *Cid* spurred Corneille to measure himself henceforth only against the very greatest poets of all time. It brought him, in like fashion, to turn away from comedy and tragicomedy, and to turn toward tragedy, tragedy being the noblest of all the dramatic genres. Nor was he content to rectify great poetic texts that had come down to him from the past. Such was the extent of his daring that he undertook in addition to rectify the traditional concept of tragedy itself. According to the inherited view, tragedy concerned a flawed hero (neither all good, nor all bad) who experienced a fall from prosperity to misfortune, exciting in the audience the emotions of pity and fear. The first change Corneille made was to replace the flawed hero with a perfect (a virtually perfect) hero, in *Polyeucte*. Then he discarded the traditional plot in favor of a dichotomous plot (good versus bad) together with a double reversal at the denouement, in *Pompée*. (He continued to speak of pity and fear in connection with his new tragedies, but it is clear that they often excite awe—or *admiration*—also, as he himself finally admitted in the dedicatory letter for *Nicomède*.) The means by which Corneille effected this rectification are obvious: he found in the *Discorsi* of Tasso traditional contrastive definitions of the two genres, with stress on the perfection of the epic hero, and he conceived the idea of rectifying tragedy by making tragedy more like epic. There are no doubt other reasons why Corneille gravitated toward epic texts just after the Quarrel of the *Cid*. Tasso and Vergil had both figured in the argument of the Quarrel: Tasso as the greatest modern poet, whom Corneille might (Chapelain) or might not (Scudéry) be able to emulate; Vergil, as guarantor of the poet's right to modify any literary or historical text he wants, provided only that (unlike Vergil) he make changes always in the direction of the ethically better. Like Tasso, Corneille had seen a poem of his become the center of a major literary debate, involving not just individuals but an academy; like Vergil, he was criticized for having created an unworthy heroine. (The Vergilian Dido was unworthy of the real historical Dido; Corneille's Chimène, true to the facts of history, was unworthy of modern audiences.) The overriding factor in Corneille's preoccupation with epic at this point in his career, however, must have been the desire to refashion tragedy. Refashioning tragedy would be a major accomplishment, on the scale of Tasso's own accomplishment in Christianizing the epic. He could lay claim to having done for tragedy what Tasso had done for the epic; and by this emulation he would have advanced the development of poetry as a whole, releasing tragedy from its second-class heroic status and bringing about the final perfection of heroic poetry in general. It was only after this new vision of tragedy was in place that the playwright began to correct dramatic texts.

The progression of the plays within the trilogy seems to recapitulate Tasso's theory of the evolutionary succession of great epic poem-types, from the archaic *Iliad* to the refined but still pagan *Aeneid* to the modern, Christian epic (like the *Gerusalemme*, which Tasso out of modesty does not mention). To the extent that the trilogy constitutes the sum of all previous epics (that is, all first-class heroic poetry) and at the same time transcends the limitations formerly imposed on tragedy (as second-class heroic poetry), it constitutes a real *summa eroica*. The Mazarin cabinet, with its portraits of Homer, Vergil, Tasso, and Corneille, celebrated the succession of great heroic poets across time and space. It did not, insofar as one can tell from descriptions, convey the whole of the dialectical relationship among these poets, however; it simply asserted succession without explaining by what modes succession had taken place. The trilogy, if the reading I have proposed is right, goes much farther: it shows that epic poetry has served to perfect tragedy, and that in turn this new tragedy serves to perfect heroic poetry as a whole.

It is one thing to forge a new concept of tragedy; it is another thing to live with and to use it. At the end of *Polyeucte*, Corneille had completed the perfecting of the tragic hero; at the end of *Pompée*, he had completed the plot structure of the new tragedy. In the "trilogie des monstres," he takes the end of *Polyeucte* and the end of *Pompée* as a starting point. The new plot structure seems not to have given him any trouble, but the new hero did. A hero not on his way to perfection, but already in possession of perfection, turned out to yield little in the way of dramatic interest. Corneille himself commented on the problem in connection with the most perfect of these perfect heroes, Théodore:

> [Le caractère] de Théodore est entièrement froid: elle n'a au-
> cune passion qui l'agite; et là même où son zèle pour Dieu,
> qui occupe toute son âme, devroit éclater le plus, c'est-à-dire
> dans sa contestation avec Didyme pour le martyre, je lui ai
> donné si peu de chaleur, que cette scène, bien que très courte,
> ne laisse pas d'ennuyer. Ainsi, pour en parler sainement, une
> vierge et martyre sur un théâtre n'est autre chose qu'un Terme
> qui n'a ni jambes ni bras, et par conséquent point d'action.
> (Examen of *Théodore, Oeuvres,* 5:12)

The problem was solved by giving to the antihero the task of carrying the play, with the result that *Rodogune, Théodore,* and

Héraclius can be said to constitute a "trilogie des monstres." In some respects *Rodogune* is a mirror image of *Polyeucte*. Cléopâtre dominates the action as Polyeucte had in the earlier work. Both set a challenge to the other characters in the play; both are absent from act 3 (so too are Horace and Auguste), as the other characters react to that challenge. Cléopâtre goes down in defeat, however, whereas Polyeucte triumphed and carried the other characters to triumph along with him. *Rodogune* shifts the focus from good to evil, but otherwise changes nothing. The new tragedy remains a providential tragedy, centered on the clash between good (virtually perfect) characters and bad (or evil) characters. From *Rodogune* to *Théodore* to *Héraclius,* Corneille does gradually decrease the evilness of the antihero; and this evolution away from the almost absolute evil of Cléopâtre results eventually in a modification of the double reversal (the triumph of the good and the defeat of the bad). This occurs outside the present frame of reference—in *Nicomède,* which ends with the repentance and reintegration into society of the antihero, Arsinoé. The "trilogie des monstres" offers considerable aesthetic satisfaction, particularly *Rodogune*. It does not, however, have the sweep or the incisiveness of the Roman trilogy, perhaps because Corneille's major effort lay behind him. To put it another way, the Roman trilogy draws strength from the fact that the poet and his heroes were engaged in the simultaneous pursuit of much the same kind of heroic goal: to break through to a new higher level of ethical and/or aesthetic truth. That sort of concatenation, almost by definition, cannot be expected to repeat itself; and, in Corneille's case, it did not.

Corneille was a modern before the Quarrel of the *Cid*. One can see it above all perhaps in his insistence on positing pleasure as the primary aim of the theater and positing contemporary audiences as arbiters of the playwright's success. After the Quarrel, he remained a modern, but he considerably modified the modernism with which he had started out. In his greatest plays, he is a modern in much the same way that Tasso had been a modern: he venerates the pagan heritage and draws on it to a greater extent than before, but at the same time he wants to renew and to complete that heritage by infusing it with a new, Christian ethics and a corresponding new, Christian aesthetics.

The story of Corneille's emulation of Tasso connects with

several important areas of previous Cornelian scholarship: with studies on providentialism in his theater (Maurens, Poirier, Stegmann, Sweetser); with the groundbreaking article by Marc Fumaroli on *Rodogune* as the work of a Christian humanist "correcting" the Ancients' view of man and tragedy; with the same author's numerous contributions to the history of Italian cultural and intellectual influences in seventeenth-century France; finally, with approaches to Corneille's theater that emphasize the dialectical relationship of the plays one to the other (Sweetser, Doubrovsky). Emulation was for Corneille a powerfully integrative act; studying that emulation, I hope, has in turn provided the occasion for bringing various aspects of previous knowledge about Corneille into new, sharper focus.

There remains the question of how to judge Corneille's silence about his debt to Tasso and, even more, his reticence about having created a form of Christian art at all. I suggested earlier that considerations of prudence may initially have dictated a policy of silence. In setting out to emulate Tasso, Corneille was aiming exceptionally high; if he were to publicize the fact, he might only make it easier for his critics to attack him again. The weight of such an argument would have diminished with the passage of time, however. But as the playwright began to feel himself coming closer and closer to achieving his original goal, pride could have taken over from prudence as a motive for continuing silence. In the "Excuse à Ariste," Corneille had exulted in his own independence: "Je ne dois qu'à moy seul toute ma Renommée"; and Mairet had promptly taken him to task for the transparency of his dependence on Guillén de Castro in the *Cid*. Perhaps the debt toward Tasso came in the end to seem too great for acknowledgment simply because to acknowledge it might detract from the playwright's legitimate accomplishments, which were to have dared to emulate Tasso in the first place and to have succeeded in the second. These motives, it seems to me, are both plausible and, if not noble, at least respectable.[1]

If we look at the problem from another angle, it is possible, I think, to say more. Corneille was trying to combine elements of the sacred and the profane somewhat as Tasso had done in the *Gerusalemme liberata*. The authority of the *Gerusalemme* went unchallenged in France insofar as epic poetry was concerned, but Corneille could not automatically transfer that authority to the theater. The theater had recently reformed itself, thrown off its old licentiousness, and become a place where even decent women might safely go. Corneille calls attention to the fact in the final scene of *L'Illusion comique*; and in creating a modern, basically Christian form of tragedy, he no doubt hoped to push that reform still further. There were limits beyond which he could not go, however. A cloud of moral ambiguity still hung over the theater, and it would continue to hang there for the rest of the century. The power of the theater to move its audience was a fact recognized by friend and foe alike. It was a power that derived from the mode of dramatic imitation itself: imitation of an action by means of representation or reenactment by living actors. Such was the fear of the theater's special rhetoric of persuasion that the strict moralists condemned it outright (and thought that the better the play was aesthetically, the more corruptive it was likely to be morally). Those of more worldly inclinations entered eagerly into the theatrical illusion, but did not expect or want to find a great deal more than confirmation of the grandeur, the pleasures, and the pains of this world. This is the audience for which Corneille wrote, the audience which he said it was his purpose to please, not instruct. He was too dependent on this audience, too respectful of its prejudices, ever to think of assaulting its expectations head-on. The conditions were not right in France for transposing Tassoan modenism directly into dramatic terms. All things considered, one should perhaps wonder then not that Corneille concealed so much, but that he dared to go so far and reveal so much.

NOTES

1. *La Suivante* was published in early September 1637. The Quarrel had broken out in March and would not reach its official end until the publication of the *Sentiments* in December. The Academy had entered the debate toward the end of May and was deliberating still when Corneille wrote the dedicatory letter for *La Suivante*.

2. These translations are due, for the most part, to Jean Baudoin (JB) and Vion d'Alibray (V d'A):

Ierusalem deslivree, 1626 (JB)

Les Morales du Tasse, 1632 (JB)

L'Esprit, ou l'Ambassadeur, le Secretaire, et le Père de famille, 1632 (JB)

L'Aminte, 1632 (V d'A)

L'Aminte, 1632 (Rayssiguier)

La Ierusalem, 2d ed., 1632 (JB)

De la Noblesse: Dialogue, 1633 (JB)

Torrismon, 1636 (V d'A)

"Du Poëme heroïque," in *Recueil d'emblemes divers*, pp. 577–619, 1639 (JB)

Tasso's prestige in France is attested by many scholars, including Beall, Simpson, Adam, Bray, and Maskell (in works cited in the Bibliography).

3. See the Au Lecteur (unpaginated) for *Le Torrismon du Tasse*. D'Alibray does not identify Beni, Du Bartas, and Balzac by name, but he obviously counts on the reader to know whom he is quoting. He slightly modifies the quotation from Du Bartas, which should read: "Le Toscane est fondé sur . . . / Le Tasse, digne ouvrier d'un Heroique vers, / Figuré, court, aigu, limé, riche en langage, / *Et premier en bonneur, bien que dernier en âge*" (Beall, p. 16). On the question of Corneille's possible relationship to d'Alibray, see chapter 6, note 8.

4. The correspondence was first uncovered and analyzed by René Pintard in an article cited by Mongrédien.

5. The critic Colbert Searles ("Italian Influences as seen in the Sentiments of the French Academy on the *Cid*") concludes that *Les Sentiments de l'Academie Françoise sur le Cid* must, in view of its great influences upon French classic literature, be regarded as one of the most considerable vehicles by which Italian literary doctrines and Italian methods of criticism have ever been brought into France" (p. 388).

6. These same four literary quarrels are analyzed in detail by Bernard Weinberg in vol. 2 of his *History of Literary Criticism in the Italian Renaissance*.

7. His exact words are: "Car les passions violentes bien exprimées, font souvent en ceux qui les voyent une partie de l'effect, qu'elles font en ceux qui les ressentent veritablement. Elles ostent à tous la liberté de l'esprit, et font que les uns se plaisent à voir representer les fautes, que les autres se plaisent à commettre. Ce sont ces puissans mouvemens, qui ont tiré des Spectateurs du Cid cette grande approbation, et qui doivent aussi la faire excuser. L'Autheur s'est facilement rendu maistre de leur ame, apres y avoir excité le trouble et l'esmotion; leur esprit flatté par quelques endroits agreables, est devenu aisément flateur de tout le reste, et les charmes esclatans de quelques parties leur ont donné de l'amour pour tout le corps" (Gasté, p. 414).

8. Corneille may also have written the "Lettre du des-interessé au Sieur Mairet," which stakes out a position somewhere between the "Advertissement" and the dedicatory letter for *La Suivante*. It condescends to Mairet unsparingly, but it also invokes the ideal of "une honnête émulation" among poets and interprets Corneille's silence as a sign of "modération" (Gasté, pp. 313, 318).

9. "Volesse Iddio, illustrissimo ed eccelentissimo principe, che il mio poema o non fosse stato soggeto ad alcune opposizioni, o non avesse ritrovato l'oppositore; ma poi che l'una è imperfezione dell'arte umana, la qual non può far cosa perfetta; l'altra della nostra natura, la qual fa gli uomini men pronti al lodare che al biasimare, debbo ringraziarlo che, se mi son negate l'altrui lodi, non mi sian mancate le mie difese: le quali ho roccolte en questa operetta, che porta in fronte il titolo d'*Apologia*" (pp. 65–66).

10. Tasso and Corneille arrived at their common position from different directions, Tasso having started out with the idea of appealing to a more or less erudite audience and having realized only later the need to appeal if possible to a broader audience as well. H. B. Charlton, in *Castelvetro's Theory of Poetry*, cites a statement of Tasso's that is close to what Corneille says in the dedication of *La Suivante*. Whether Corneille actually read this text, I cannot say. "Io per me come che sommamente ammiri la dottrina e l'altezza d'ingegno di Guido Cavalcanti, e di Dante in particolare . . . non dimeno stimo che la strada tenuta da loro, siccome è più nova, e men calcata dell'altre, così non sia quella, che ci conduce a quell'eterna gloria, che dal consenso universale di tutti gli uomini, e di tutti i secoli, alli eccellenti poeti è apparecchiata" (Charlton, p. 75; quoted from *Lezione nell'accademia ferrarese*).

CHAPTER II

1. Gérard Genette, in *Palimpsestes: la littérature au second degré*, propose the terms "transposition homodiégétique" and "transposition hétérodiégétique" for categories much like the ones I have in mind here (pp. 340–50).

2. Corneille probably read Euripides in Latin. The version cited here is that of George Buchanan, in his *Poemata quae extant* (Leyden, 1628).

   (a) Hippolyte:
   Quelle tendre amitié je recevois d'un père!
   Je l'ai quitté pourtant pour suivre ta misère;
   Et je tendis les bras à mon enlèvement,
   Ne pouvant être à toi de son consentement.

   (ll. 1397–1400)

Medea:

     . . . prodito patre & domo,
Applicui Iolchon te sequuta, tibi nimis
Hic obsecundans, ac mihi parum providens.

(pp. 462–63)

(b) Hippolyte:

Si pour te voir heureux ta foi s'est relâchée,
Rends-moi dedans le sein dont tu m'as arrachée.
Je t'aime, et mon amour m'a fait tout hasarder.
Non pas pour tes grandeurs, mais pour te posséder.

(ll. 1405–8)

Medea:

Quo nunc revertar? spreta quo me conferam?
An ad penates patrios, ac patriam,
Quam te sequuta prodidi?

(p. 463)

(c) Théagène:

Ne me reproche plus ta fuite ni ta flamme:
Que ne fait point l'amour quand il possède une âme?
Son pouvoir à ma vue attachoit tes plaisirs,
Et tu me suivois moins que tes propres desirs.

(ll. 1409–12)

Jason:

Ingenii acumen acre suppetit tibi: at
Orationis arrogans jactantia est,
Ea quum recenses, quae coacta feceras
Amore, duris nos ut è laboribus
Eruere posses.

(p. 463)

(d) Théagène (who now occupies a high position in society):

Regrette maintenant ton père et ses richesses;
Fâche-toi de marcher à côté des princesses;
Retourne en ton pays avecque tous tes biens
Chercher un rang pareil à celui que tu tiens.

(ll. 1421–24)

Jason:

At, ut docebo te, incolumitate ex mea
Plus quam dedisti, ad te redundat commodi.
Primum, Pelasgam, patria pro barbara,
Terram colis, ubi lex & aequitas vigent,
Nec jura cedunt gratiae vel viribus:
Omnesque doctam te esse Graii intelligunt:
Famaque flores, finibus si in ultimis
Orbis habitares, mentio haud fieret tui.

(p. 464)

(e) Théagène:

Les femmes, à vrai dire, ont d'étranges esprits!
Qu'un mari les adore, et qu'une amour extrême

A leur bigearre [sic] humeur le soumette lui-mesme,
Qu'il les comble d'honneurs et de bons traitements,
Qu'il ne refuse rien à leurs contentements:
Fait-il la moindre brèche à la foi conjugale,
Il n'est point à leur gré de crime qui l'égale;
C'est vol, c'est perfidie, assassinat, poison,
C'est massacrer son père, et brûler sa maison.

(ll. 1428–36)

Jason:

At eo mulierum crevit impotentia:
Si conjugalis salva sit fides tori,
Tum cuncta recte creditis succedere:
Sin hac sinistre parte quidquam evenerit,
Quae cara fuerant, sunt statim inimicissima.
At quam fuisset procreasse liberos
Aliunde melius, nec fuisse foeminas?
Exempta quantis vita foret hominum malis.

(p. 464)

(f) Théagène:

Crois-tu qu'aucun respect ou crainte du trépas
Puisse obtenir sur moi ce que tu n'obtiens pas?
Dis que je suis ingrat, appelle-moi parjure;
Mais à nos feux sacrés ne fais plus tant d'injure:
Ils conservent encor leur première vigueur.

(ll. 1463–67)

Jason:

Non (quod tibi aegre est) quod torū odissem tuum,
Sponsaeque amore saucius forem novae,
Nec numero ut ulli liberûm contenderem:
Sat liberorum est. . . .

(p. 464)

(g) Hippolyte:

Puisque mon teint se fane et ma beauté se passe,
Il est bien juste aussi que ton amour se lasse.

(ll. 1497–98)

Medea:

Non haec movebat causa te, sed barbaras
Taedas senectam adusque fore putaveras
Parum decoras.

(p. 465)

3. Couton, *Corneille*, p. 48, says "L'essentiel de la discussion porte sur la conduite de Chimène épousant le meurtrier de son père." See also Maurens, *La Tragédie sans tragique*, p. 248.

4. Marie-Odile Sweetser has linked *Polyeucte* to book 4 of the *Aeneid*, and more especially Pauline to Dido, in two illuminating articles devoted to the figure of the abandoned woman in ancient literature and in modern French (seventeenth-century) literature. The focus of the first article is on a generalized moral evolution whereby heroines like Pauline, Bérénice, and Marianne,

in comparison to Dido, Medea, and Ariadne, are seen to control their passions through the exercise of "les facultés supérieures, intelligence et volonté, généralement considérées comme l'apanage de l'homme ou du héros en littérature" ("La Femme abandonnée: esquisse d'une typologie," p. 169). A more recent article ("Images de la femme abandonnée: traditions, contaminations, créations") views the problem anew from the perspective of Christian humanist syncretism: "Ce sont des poètes chrétiens et modernes qui transforment cet abandon subi en séparation consentie et qui créent une nouvelle figure de femme, capable de s'élever au même niveau de grandeur et de sacrifice que l'homme" (p. 9). In this last context, Sweetser argues that Pauline plays as important a role as Polyeucte in ensuring their ultimate reunion in God: "En refusant d'abandonner Polyeucte [quand celui-ci la quitte pour le martyre], Pauline l'amène à comprendre que lui non plus ne peut ni ne doit l'abandonner, que la foi chrétienne doit les réunir, non les séparer. L'abandon se transforme alors en une union en Dieu, en une véritable apothéose 'cum sanctis tuis in aeternum' " (p. 8). See also the same critic's "Place de l'amour dans la hiérarchie des valeurs chrétiennes," especially pp. 73–76.

5. I have used the Pease edition of book 4 of the *Aeneid* (Cambridge: Harvard University Press, 1935).

6. The English text is that of Rolfe Humphries (New York: Scribner's, 1951).

7. As we shall see later, it is in fact the "historical" or "chaste" Dido, as distinct from the Vergilian heroine, who serves as the model for Pauline at this point in the play. The discovery and promotion by Christian moralists of this other Dido represents an important early stage of the syncretism invoked by Marie-Odile Sweetser in her article "Images de la femme abandonnée." In addition to Sweetser, at least two other critics have suggested a parallel between Dido and Pauline. Jean Guitton, "Aspects religieux," p. 25, contrasts Pauline with several famous heroines including Dido: "Elle se distingue de ces héroïnes célèbres, de ces femmes toujours plus ou moins *possédées*, quand ce seroit par l'idéal. Comme l'a noté Sainte-Beuve, on oublie de citer (à côté d'Antigone, de Didon, de Béatrice, d'Ophélie ou de Phèdre) cette épouse raisonnable, cette femme *dépossédée* et par là préchrétienne, chez qui la douce fidélité s'élève par degrés jusqu'à la foi conjugale." The reference to Sainte-Beuve is presumably to a passage in an essay on Stendhal (*Causeries du lundi*, 9:336) dealing with the contrast between *amour-passion* (deemed by Stendhal virtually nonexistent in France) and what Sainte-Beuve calls "l'amour à la française, mélange d'attrait physique sans doute, mais aussi de goût et d'inclination morale, de galanterie délicate, d'estime, d'enthousiasme, de raison même et d'esprit, un amour où il reste un peu de sens commun, où la société n'est pas oubliée entièrement, où le devoir n'est pas sacrifié à l'aveugle et ignoré. Pauline, dans Corneille, me représente bien l'idéal de cet amour, où l'élévation et l'honneur se font entendre. On en trouverait, en descendant, d'autres exemples compatibles avec l'agrément et une certaine décence dans la vie, amour ou liaison, ou attachement respectueux et tendre, peu importe le nom. L'amour-passion, tel que me l'ont peint dans Médée, dans Phèdre ou dans Didon, des chantres immortels, est touchant à voir grâce à eux, et j'en admire le tableau: mais cet amour-passion, devenu systématique chez Bayle, m'impatiente. . . . "

8. Vergil compares Aeneas to an oak during the scene with Anna, sent by Dido to make a second effort to detain Aeneas. As Pease notes, some critics argue that Aeneas does shed tears in front of Anna (l. 449), though his resolve remains unshaken. In any event, if Aeneas weeps and if Anna notices it, she says nothing about it. Pauline's pointed reference, on the other hand, calls attention to Polyeucte's tears. This is perhaps Corneille's way of underscoring the *difference* between his play and the *Aeneid.*

9. A passage in the "Discours de la tragédie" (*Oeuvres,* 1:75–76) suggests that Corneille associated the Ancients' frequent use of divine agents to complicate or resolve plots with their failure to distinguish clearly between myth and history. It is proper, he says, to introduce Venus into the action of a play like *Andromède,* since the subject there is mythological; it would have been ridiculous, however, to introduce Jupiter into *Nicomède,* Mercury into *Cinna,* or an angel into *Héraclius* (the historical era of the last play being Christian). Corneille does not consider other options that he might have brought up: for example, a biblical play or a miracle play, in which the appearance of an angel would presumably be as appropriate as that of a god in a Greek or Roman play. In fact, he mentions only mythological plays and historical plays, presumably because these were types he found in the contemporary French theater. (There would, of course, have been some problem with staging the descent of an angel, but no more so than with the descent of pagan divinities in machine plays like *Andromède* and *La Toison d'or.*) Corneille apparently began with the idea that *Polyeucte* belonged to the historical, as opposed to the mythological, mode. As a consequence, he felt he had to exclude any kind of divine messenger in favor of a human counterpart. At the end of the play, he is willing to tolerate the "miraculous" conversions of Pauline and Félix, on the grounds that such conversions are commonplace ("ordinaires") in the lives of saints; the descent of angelic messengers he apparently thought of as too rare an occurrence to consider belonging to the realm of history.

10. Riddle, *Genesis and Sources,* p. 59, notes that in the source cited by Corneille, Surius, the character of Sévère does not appear. Riddle suggests that Corneille might have modeled the character after Massinisse, in Mairet's *Sophonisbe,* and might have borrowed the name from Alexander Severus, a philosopher-emperor who admired the Christians but was not himself converted. (See also Poirier, *Corneille et la vertu de prudence,* p. 279.) I am inclined to think the name is also an ironic pun underscoring how lacking in "severity" this rectified version of Iarbas really is.

CHAPTER III

1. As Loukovitch makes clear (*Evolution de la tragédie religieuse,* pp. 270–95), there was considerable opposition in France to the idea of a worldly play on a religious subject. Corneille undoubtedly knew the neo-Latin theater, where religious works abounded; in the Examen of *Polyeucte,* he says, in fact, that "c'est sur ces exemples [de Heinsius, Grotius, et Buchanan] que j'ai hasardé ce poème." I would agree with Loukovitch when he says, "Ce serait une illusion de s'imaginer qu'en écrivant *Polyeucte* Corneille ait voulu braver le public" (p. 285); but it is necessary to stress that Corneille was in fact taking a risk in bringing to the worldly theater the religious themes normally reserved

for the *collèges*. Riddle (*Genesis and Sources*, p. 58) also deems Corneille's explanation in the Examen insufficient: "It is difficult to believe, however, that these plays [of Heinsius et al.], not destined for the popular stage, could have had any influence in determining Corneille's choice of a religious subject." Doubrovsky (*Corneille et la dialectique du héros*, p. 223) puts the issue clearly when he asks, "Pourquoi Corneille se serait[-il] mis soudain en tête d'écrire une 'tragédie chrétienne,' blessant par là les usages courants et les opinions prévalentes, dont il se montrait toujours si respectueux?"

2. See Pease, ed., *Aeneidos Liber Quartus*, pp. 64–67; Lancaster, *History*, pt. 2, vol. 1, pp. 346–48, who notes that Corneille mentions the plays of Scudéry and Boisrobert in the Au Lecteur of *Sophonisbe*; and Searles, "Italian Influences," p. 376 n. 12, who cites Beni and Castelvetro on the matter of flaws in the *Aeneid*: "Beni considered Virgil inferior to Tasso: 'per essersi Enea lasciato indurre da Didone ad atto dishonesto, con porgere indegno essempio al giovinetto Ascanio'. . . . Castelvetro held that the Aeneas-Dido episode "è vitiosa, perché è attione reale falsa, & riprovata dall' historia nel modo, & nel tempo. Nel modo, perche Didone per conservamento dell' honestà s'uccise, volendo servare la fede al marito morto anchora, nel tempo perche Enea non pote capitare in Africa, che Didone fosse viva.' " Tasso alludes to the controversy over Vergil's treatment of Dido in the *Discorsi del poema eroico*, pp. 103–4, and quotes three lines from Petrarch's *Trionfo della Pudicizia* in praise of Dido. Elsewhere, in an essay, Tasso meditates on the double standard whereby only women appear to be blamed for lack of chastity and excuses Dido on the ground that she was really in love with Aeneas (see the "Discorso della virtù feminile e donnesca," translated by Jean Baudoin as "De la vertu des dames illustres" and included in his *Morales du Tasse*).

3. Colbert Searles, in his article "Italian Influences as Seen in the Sentiments of the French Academy on the *Cid*," pp. 387–88, cites a very similar argument in Castelvetro: "Conciosia cosa che i poeti antichi non havessono niuno avanti loro, che loro havesse mostrata la buona via del poetare, & fosse stato loro scorta, & per conseguente sieno degni di scusa, se ciascuno di loro non ha havute tutte l'eccellenze insieme della poesia, & se quelle, le quali hanno havute, non sono in sommo grado d'eccellenza. Ma i poeti moderni, che hanno vedute, quali cose sono commendabili, & quali biasimevoli ne poeti antichi, non solamente deono prendere le parti commendabili loro, ma per loro industria debbono anchora, aggiungendovi perfettione maggiore, migliorarle, & prenderle più commendabili, senza che gli antichi non hebbero l'arte scritta di poesia, secondo la quale potessono regolare, & essaminiare i loro poemi, & la quale è proposta hora a poeti moderni, il filo della quale sequendo essi, non possono errare."

4. For the quarrel over Tasso and Ariosto, see Weinberg, *History*, 2:954–1073.

5. Actually Beni claims superiority for the *Gerusalemme* on both ethical and artistic grounds. Thus the first "Discorso" of the *Comparatione* aims to prove "che Torquato Tasso nel suo Goffredo habbia rappresentato molto più nobile e perfetta Idea di valoroso Capitano & Heroe, che Homero o Virgiliano," whereas later discourses treat of such matters as narrative unity, heroic grandeur, the use of episodes, etc. In the published commentaries on the *Gerusalemme* (first ten cantos), Beni says of Tasso: "che il suo Goffredo giunga al

sommo, e perciò e possa e debba ricerversi per ESSEMPIO & IDEA dell'HEROICO POEMA" (p. 9).

6. In 1660 Corneille was to reaffirm the viability of the concept of the tragic hero who is perfect, at least as regards Polyeucte. In the Examen of that play, he wrote: "Ceux qui veulent arrêter nos héros dans une médiocre bonté où quelques interprètes d'Aristote bornent leur vertu, ne trouveront pas ici leur compte, puisque celle de Polyeucte va jusqu'à la sainteté, et n'a aucun mélange de foiblesse"; and in the "Discours de la tragédie": "L'exclusion des personnes tout à fait vertueuses qui tombent dans le malheur bannit les martyrs de notre théâtre. *Polyeucte* y a réussi contre cette maxime. . . . " The force of these statements is somewhat attenuated, however, by his judgment elsewhere of Théodore: "Pour en parler sainement, une vierge et martyre sur un théâtre, n'est autre chose qu'un terme qui n'a ni jambes ni bras, et par conséquent point d'action" (Examen). One way or another, modern-day critics usually deny the possibility of a specifically tragic martyrdom, or of a martyr who is simultaneously a tragic hero. Stegmann accepts Polyeucte as a tragic hero, but only to the extent that the hero in him can be divorced from the martyr-saint: Polyeucte is heroic "non comme martyr, mais comme héros *tragique* dans son arrachement à Pauline, à lui-même et l'affirmation d'une hiérarchie des valeurs à l'égard de l'engagement dans le monde. C'est sa situation, sa lutte tout humaine, non son martyre qui le fait héros. Il est saint *en plus*, et ceci, pas plus que pour *Théodore* n'intéresse Corneille" ("L'Ambiguïté du concept héroïque," p. 39 n. 19). Sweetser endorses this view and adds the idea of "un tragique intérieur," supposedly characteristic of the hero but not the saint or martyr (*La Dramaturgie de Corneille*, p. 71). Doubrovsky views the play as a paradox: if Polyeucte "est un saint, c'est la théorie fondamentale de la tragédie qui a tort; et si la théorie de la tragédie n'a pas tort, c'est Polyeucte qui n'est pas un saint" (*Corneille et la dialectique du héros*, p. 223). Perhaps the essential differences between Polyeucte and Théodore lies in the fact that one is in the process of attaining a state of perfection, whereas the other is only defending a perfection that already exists. This is a distinction that Corneille himself did not make, however, at least not clearly. In any event, I think he would have opposed vigorously the idea of separating the hero and the martyr in Polyeucte and also the idea that the combination of the hero and the martyr must necessarily be paradoxical. Corneille's thought is more dialectical than it is paradoxical; and he is interested not in rejecting outright either the idea of the tragic hero or the theory of tragedy, but rather in bringing both the hero and the tragic genre to their logical point of (Christian) perfection.

CHAPTER IV

1. The critic is C. M. Bowra, as quoted by Pease, ed., *Aeneidos Liber Quartus*, p. 39 n. 295.

2. See ibid., pp. 54–55: "It is this feeling [of majestic finality] throughout the *Aeneid* which perhaps more than any other single factor differentiates it from the Homeric poems, for while the *Aeneid* takes its title from a personal hero, it is really an epic—perhaps the first in history—constructed about an abstract idea, namely the fulfillment of destiny."

3. The critic, Bruno Nardi, is quoted by Davis, p. 101.

4. Poirier mentions Dante as a possible source both for the general idea of the trilogy and for the specific subject of *Horace* (pp. 45–46). He does not, however, see Dante as a link between Corneille and Vergil (a crucial point in my argument), but only as another in a great number of moral philosophers on whom the playwright may have drawn for inspiration.

5. I use the term *heroic decorum* to emphasize the connection between the moral ascent of Corneille's heroes in the trilogy and the theory of heroic poetry found in the *Discorsi* of Tasso. Poirier, for his part, links this ascent with "le schéma très classique de la Triple-Voie renouvelé du schéma grec des trois genres de vie" and mentions in this regard not only Plato and Aristotle, but Paul, Augustine, Thomas, and Bonaventure, as well as (closer to Corneille) Ficino, Lefèvre d'Etaples, Bellarmin, and J.-P. Camus (pp. 47–48).

6. Tasso also was thought to have summarized the past, as one can see from the quatrain published under the poet's engraved portrait in the *Morales du Tasse* of 1632:

> C'est icy le portrait, l'exemple et le sommaire
>   Des plus rares Esprits;
> Mais l'immortel crayon de Virgile, et d'Homère,
>   Se voit dans ses Escrits.

CHAPTER V

1. For a summary of divergent views, see Gérard, pp. 323–24.

2. Achorée has a fairly long but purely functional role. Charged with delivering lengthy accounts of the murder of Pompée, of César's reaction to the crime, and finally of the death of Ptolomée, he invariably speaks either to Cléopâtre or to her surrogate, Charmion. He is himself a surrogate of the queen, and the content of his *récits* always corresponds perfectly to the interpretation that Cléopâtre herself would give of the events in question. Being entirely without will or goals of his own, Achorée is totally devoid of what we call character. He is neither a sycophantic servant nor another "good" Egyptian; he is only a dramatic function. He reflects Cléopâtre's point of view.

3. Butler looks on the denouement as expressing a "justice immanente" through the misfortune that befalls all the Machiavellian characters (pp. 180, 186, 219); several other critics, like Nelson (p. 129) and Vedel (p. 124), without specifically mentioning the denouement, treat the whole play as a straightforward confrontation between the noble and the ignoble (with all the ignoble punished at the end). The ambiguity of the play and the denouement is stressed by Doubrovsky (p. 281), Barnwell (pp. 201–3), and Pavel (pp. 54–62). Gérard finds that the play ends ambiguously if one stops with the final scene (which he says shows César and Cléopâtre in a state of undeserved triumph) but that it nevertheless suggests poetic justice because references in the dialogue to the future course of history remind the audience that the triumph will be short-lived (pp. 344–45). Sweetser provides the most accurate reading by speaking not only of a "dénouement moral" (involving Cléopâtre and Ptolomée) but also of a "dénouement ambigu" (rising out of Cornélie's view of the future). Sweetser notes the presence of these two denouements but does not attempt to explain how they come to occur side by side in the same play

(*Dramaturgie*, p. 127). Voltaire belongs to neither of these critical persuasions, having little or no interest in the play's ethical implications. The logical denouement, he thinks, occurs when Ptolomée dies, and the scenes that follow are not so much ambiguous as unaesthetic because useless (comments on 5. 3–4). He sees Cornélie's frequent reminders that she intends to avenge Pompée's death on César not as contributing in any substantial way to the plot but rather as inconsistency of characterization. If she admires and trusts César, why does she carry on at such length about her hopes of causing his death later on (comments on 4. 4, and 5. 1, 2, and 4)?

4. Voltaire says that because *Pompée* has little or no plot it is probably not a tragedy but that it nevertheless contains brilliant scenes, termed "hors-d'oeuvres" and "beaux morceaux" (comments on 3. 3–4; 4. 4; and 5. 1 and 5). Similar views have been expressed more recently by Nelson (p. 129), May (pp. 35–36), and Vedel (pp. 124–25).

5. Several critics suggest that Corneille wrote *Pompée* as a veiled attack on Richelieu, who he thought had exercised a pernicious influence over Louis XIII. (See May, pp. 34–43; Adam, *Histoire*, 2:363; Couton, p. 105; and Maurens, pp. 304–9.) It seems likely to me that the playwright turned to the *Pharsalia* primarily for aesthetic reasons, then discovered and decided to exploit the possibility of reference to the then current political situation in France. Contemporary audiences no doubt saw the parallel in any event, and when Corneille came to dedicate the play (to Richelieu's successor, Mazarin), he took steps to forestall any comparison between Mazarin and the Egyptian advisers. Another point: just as Richelieu was said to be Machiavellian, so Ptolomée and his council have often been described as following policies of duplicity and expediency set forth in *The Prince*. (See Doubrovsky, pp. 273–81; Stegmann, *Héroïsme*, 2:299, 591; and Butler, pp. 169–71.) From this point of view, too, the play seems to show allusions that are easily contained within the Tassoan scheme of "fideli" vs. "infideli."

6. Cornélie's leap of faith is of course in no way binding on the audience, anymore than it is on her. Both may continue to doubt César's motives. At one or two crucial points, however, Cornélie feels compelled to act on one or another assumption concerning César; and when this happens, the audience in turn is compelled to assess the ethics of her choice. If the evidence were overwhelmingly favorable to César, the audience would view Cornélie's decision to "believe" as virtually inescapable or necessary; if the evidence were overwhelmingly unfavorable, the audience would view her decision as arbitrary and radically out of touch with reality. In the circumstances prevailing in *Pompée*, the spectator need only judge that Cornélie is faced with an ethical dilemma that she clearly appreciates as such and that she courageously chooses to confront rather than to evade. César's "character" remains as problematical as ever. Garnier's *Cornélie* (1574) deals with some of the same events as *Pompée*, but from a different perspective and for a different purpose, the earlier play being a mournful meditation on political fortune and misfortune, the later work a study of personal commitment in a universe of ethical uncertainties. César's political ambitions, paramount in *Cornélie*, are scarcely mentioned in *Pompée*. The motivation behind his expression of grief at the death of his rival is crucial in *Pompée*, where Cornélie must decide whether to intervene to protect César from the Egyptians, but of no consequence at all in the Garnier play, where the two great Romans never meet.

7. The Tassoan context referred to here is that of the *Discorsi*, in the passage cited earlier. The *Gerusalemme* elaborates a more complex and more problematical conception of love; see Greene, pp. 208–14.

8. Barnwell (pp. 31–32, 201–2) and Gérard (p. 337) see love as a humanizing weakness in César.

9. The similarity between the view of love in act 4 of *Pompée* and that in seventeenth-century novels does not necessarily mean, as Voltaire and others have assumed, that Corneille was directly influenced by contemporary novels. The novel and the modern Christian epic shared much the same ethos concerning love, and Tasso himself says in the *Discorsi* that he sees no essential difference between the "romanzo" (as exemplified by the *Orlando furioso*) and the epic poem (pp. 128–32).

10. Cléopâtre's character has three principal aspects: she is *amoureuse, ambitieuse*, and *généreuse*. In the Examen, Corneille mentions only the first two. Arguing that no historical evidence exists that she was wanton and pointing out that she formed liaisons, after all, only with the two greatest political leaders of her age, Corneille feels justified in having depicted the Egyptian queen as "amoureuse d'ambition," a woman who "semble n'avoir point d'amour qu'en tant qu'il peut servir à sa grandeur." What he neglects to say, perhaps because it would have entailed a recourse to something other than history—a recourse, in fact, to the traditions of the modern epic—is that he has actually pushed the rectifying process a step further. For if he shows that ambition governs Cléopâtre's love, he also shows that her *générosité* in turn regulates her ambition. (Ptolomée's ambition, on the contrary, is ruled by Machiavellian calculation.) He presents Cléopâtre's love, then, not as a sensual appetite but as a habit of the will; moreover, as a good, not a bad, habit of the will.

11. Barnwell has made the significant observation that the text of the play refers to Cléopâtre as "Reine" or "Princesse," never as "Madame" (p. 45).

12. The relative failure of the scene between César and Cléopâtre, together with the traditional iconography associated with Cornélie's role, may tend to blur the dramatic balance that I am suggesting Corneille intended. Herland points out that Cornélie's lamentations in act 5 quickly give way to her desire for vengeance: "Bien loin donc d'être une déploration sur la mort de Pompée, ce discours de Cornélie n'est qu'un magnifique refus de pleurer" (p. 9). Just when the playwright seems about to resurrect the old tragedy of *déploration*, he turns aside. Engravings of Cornélie with the urn, however, always evoke the first—and least important—of the characteristics she embodies in the play. What is dominant in the role as written is the combination of stoical resolve and occasional openness to faith. This view of the role does not deny the grandeur of her love for, and fidelity to, her husband; but, in the economy of the play, it is the love of César and Cléopâtre that gets the greater emphasis and that, as we have seen, opens up new ethical perspectives.

13. Doubrovsky expresses in rather abstract philosophical terms the same tensions between the ideal and the real that I have connected with Tasso and Lucan or history. Thus: "Ce qui caractérise *La Mort de Pompée*, c'est son *inachèvement*, au sens où la pièce appelle vainement une synthèse vivante de la royauté impuissante et de la puissance anti-royale, du Roi et du Romain—ainsi

que l'union concrète des Romains entre eux. . . . . [S]i *La Mort de Pompée* marque, pour le projet héroïque, la retombée de l'intemporel au temporel, le cours de l'histoire, un instant suspendu, est rétabli" (p. 281).

14. Sweetser asks several pertinent questions without venturing answers: "Faut-il en conclure à une évolution philosophique du dramaturge vers le pessimisme ou à une évolution esthétique vers un style plus réaliste? Ou constater que la vie de César et celle de Cléopâtre étaient trop connues pour permettre de changer les données historiques en créant un dénouement conforme à la formule habituelle de la réconciliation?" (*Dramaturgie*, p. 131).

CHAPTER VI

1. A pagan character in act 2, scene 1, calls her a cruel nymph; Didimo refers to her variously as "quella modesta Ninfa" (2. 5) and "quella/Ninfa di Paradiso, Angel terreno" (4. 3).

2. See Fumaroli, "Classicisme français et culture italienne," pp. 209–10. If Tasso borrows from the legend of Theodora for the Olindo-Sophronia episode, Bartolommei borrows back from the *Gerusalemme* for his modernized version of the saint's story. Bartolommei imagines that Didimo is not yet a Christian when he enters the brothel to exchange places with Teodora; and he has Teodora, before she leaves, baptize Didimo with some water held in the helmet she is to wear in escaping—an obvious variation on the scene in Tasso (12. 67) where Tancred baptizes the dying Clorinda (ibid., p. 213).

3. The mixture of pastoral and Christian elements had produced a similar widening of the gamut of types of love before Corneille. On the one hand, as noted above, the theme of carnal love had been introduced into several dramatic versions of the Theodora story. On the other, according to Fumaroli, Bonarelli had adumbrated a higher, divine stage of love in the context of pastoral itself (see "Corneille, lecteur de la *Filli di Sciro*," pp. 316–17). My interest here is not to connect Corneille with either of these aspects of the tradition combining pastoral and Christian themes, but rather to concentrate on detailing specific echoes of the *Aminta* in *Théodore*.

4. *Théodore* is not the only play in which Corneille transposes pastoral themes to a Christian, tragic mode. *Polyeucte, Rodogune,* and *Théodore* all contain interesting analogues of the "doppio amore" experienced by Celia in Bonarelli's famous pastoral (see Fumaroli, "Corneille, lecteur de la *Filli di Sciro*"). Because it is focused so directly on the *Aminta* (which it is intended to rectify and so to surpass), *Théodore*, however, certainly represents the playwright's most sustained effort to Christianize the pastoral.

5. See the contrast between Guarini's evocation of the Golden Age (*Pastor fido*, Chorus ending act 4) and Tasso's (*Aminta*, Chorus concluding act 1).

6. Fonteny's *Galathee* (1690) is an adaptation of the *Aminta*; concerning the fountain scene, see Simpson, pp. 56–57. Belliard's *Aminte* (1596), Du Mas's *Lydie* (1609), and Rayssiguier's *Aminte* (1632) stage the incidents at the fountain, respectively, in 3. 6; 2. 2; and 3. 1–3. *Amynte*, an anonymous version sometimes attributed to its publisher, T. Quinet, appeared in 1638 and likewise *showed* the scene that Tasso had rendered indirectly through narration (see

Lancaster, pt. 2, vol. 1, p. 248). Simpson points out (p. 89) that Gombaud's *Amaranthe* (1631) "met en récit la scène de la fontaine, comme le Tasse l'avait faite," but this practice is clearly not the rule but the exception.

7. Attempts to rehabilitate *Théodore* have usually been based on one of two arguments: either that, in spite of its offensive subject, the play is at least very well constructed, or else that the subject is in fact not really offensive. Important critics like Fumaroli, Sweetser, and Stegmann, all of whom rate *Théodore* higher than I do, in my opinion fail to take into account the extent to which Corneille's aims in the play are really self-contradictory. Elsewhere, I have suggested that the playwright's bad faith, particularly in act 4, led to a kind of parody by Molière in *L'Ecole des femmes* (see my article, "Comedy in *Théodore* and Beyond").

8. It is unclear what exactly the relationship may have been between Corneille and d'Alibray. Stegmann (*Héroïsme*, 1:49–55) calls d'Alibray, along with Tristan, an ally of Corneille's at the Marais from 1629 to 1637 and notes that Montdory's four great successes were his roles in *Médée*, the *Torrismon* of d'Alibray, Tristan's *Mariane*, and finally *Le Cid*. D'Alibray was, like Corneille, a Norman; and they had a mutual friend in Saint-Amant and perhaps also in Pascal. (D'Alibray had close ties with the Pascal family during the time they were living in Rouen, 1639–47.) Finally d'Alibray wrote a sonnet in praise of *Polyeucte* (Mongrédien, p. 98). Stegmann concludes that the two men were fast friends (2:53). Adam, more cautious, says only that they may have been friends (*Histoire*, 1:381). In any event Corneille must have been familiar with d'Alibray's translation of Tasso's plays and, more to the point, with the two prefaces. The preface to *L'Aminte* may well have influenced Corneille's perception of the *récit* as a means of safeguarding dramatic decorum in certain instances; and, as we shall see, the preface to *Torrismon* probably alerted him to certain problems connected with excessive complication of plots. Chapelain undoubtedly played a more important role in determining Corneille's attitude toward Tasso; but with *Théodore* and *Héraclius*, d'Alibray seems to have served his colleague, perhaps his friend, as another, secondary intermediary. On the matter of d'Alibray's own modernism, as marked in its own way as the modernism of Corneille and Chapelain or of Tasso himself, see the article of Daniela Dalla Valle, "*Le Torrismon du Tasse* par Charles Vion d'Alibray: entre tragédie et tragicomédie."

CHAPTER VII

1. Chapelain and Corneille, for all their interest in raising poetry above the level of mere illusion, continue to refer to the theater as "l'Art des beaux mensonges" and "l'aimable imposture" (Gasté, p. 416; *Oeuvres*, 6:123). A passage in the *Discorsi* may help clarify the issue (pp. 86–91). (Chapelain and Corneille could not have read the passage, since the printer inadvertently dropped it and it has only been restored in modern editions.) It is a complicated argument involving answers to Plato and Mazzone. In short, Tasso distinguishes between two types of poetry: the icastic, dealing with the real (and related to dialectics) and the phantastic, dealing with the unreal (and related to sophistry). The poet creates "imagini"—"idoli" is the corresponding term in quotations from Mazzone. But the icastic poet creates images of what exists; the

phantastic poet, images of what does not exist. Moreover, the icastic poet's images may be images either of what exists and is visible or of what exists but is not visible. Dante, he argues, is an icastic poet who deals with truth, but truth often in an invisible (mystical or allegorical) mode. When Corneille, in the "Vers à Foucquet," speaks of his art as "l'aimable imposture," he probably means only that the Auguste or Pompée on stage is not literally Augustus or Pompey. The dramatist does not literally bring the dead back from their graves. He only creates an image of Augustus or Pompey. It is an icastic image, however, inasmuch as it is an image of something that actually exists, or existed. But even this is not enough, for Corneille speaks in the same poem of wanting to add new luster to the old images of heroes found in Homer or Vergil or even his own earlier theater. Can icastic poetry be idealistic? Yes, indeed. The truth that the poet tries to catch in each new image of the hero is not the truth already set down by historians or by earlier poets but rather the truth that lies ahead—the platonic ideal of heroism, an unseen yet definitely existent Truth toward which the dialectical movement of history is supposedly tending. In this sense the play *Polyeucte* may be an "imposture" (because it offers an "image" of reality) and at the same time mark an advance toward Truth. (On the question of idealism in French classicism, Jules Brody's article "Platonisme et classicisme" is useful.) This idealism did not survive much past the middle of the century; and La Rochefoucauld, Nicole, Racine, and others who, in Bénichou's term (in his *Morales du grand siècle*), participated in the "démolition du héros" no doubt thought that Corneille had in fact only raised up another idol and that is was their duty to destroy it. One of the most interesting studies of this rejection of Cornelian heroism is to be found in the article "Melpomène au miroir: ou la Tragédie comme héroïne," in which Marc Fumaroli, much as I am endeavoring to do here for *Horace, Polyeucte*, and *Théodore*, reads *Phèdre* as a self-reflective allegory on the theater. According to this reading, Racine reviews in *Phèdre* the options open to him as a poet, rejects both the pastoral temptation (embodied in Hippolyte and Aricie) and the Cornelian temptation to seek salvation in a false compromise (represented by Oenone) and finally chooses suicide (that is, poetic suicide or silence) along with Phèdre herself.

2. The two phases of the Quarrel actually overlapped by several months (from mid-June, when the Academy began its deliberations, to October 5, when Richelieu forbade any further exchange of broadsides among individuals). Corneille's letter to Boisrobert relating how impatiently he was waiting for the verdict of the Academy was dated 15 November. The wait—that had begun in June and that had occupied the poet's undivided attention since the beginning of October—did not end until shortly before Christmas.

3. On the centrality of Chimène's conduct in the Quarrel, see Couton (p. 48) and Maurens (p. 245).

4. See Fumaroli, "Critique et création littéraire," p. 85, and "Classicisme français et culture italienne," p. 228.

5. I am indebted to Fumaroli for details of the Rospigliosi-Barberini *Teodora* as well as for the idea that Corneille probably wrote *Théodore* in order to "faire sa Cour au Ministre" ("Critique et création littéraire," p. 84, and "Classicisme français et culture italienne," pp. 220–21, 225). It is interesting to speculate on why the play failed, and particularly on the nature of the "diverses conjonctures" to which Corneille alludes in the Epître. Fumaroli suggests that

Corneille got caught in the crosscurrents of public opinion concerning the mixture of sacred and profane elements in the theater ("Création," pp. 88–89; "Classicisme," pp. 229–35). I see another possible explanation. *Théodore* was first performed some time in 1645, when exactly we do not know. We do know that the Barberini pope, Urban VIII, died in July of 1644 and was succeeded two months later by Innocent X, widely considered to be anti-French. Mazarin was furious at the outcome of the conclave and held the Barberini nephews—Antonio and Francesco, both cardinals—partly to blame. He broke off relations with his erstwhile patrons as a consequence and was not reconciled with them until October of 1645, by which time the new pope had turned against the nephews, forcing them into exile. (My source here is Chéruel, 2:141–69.) Mazarin would eventually receive the eminent refugees very cordially in France; but out of ignorance or lack of tact, Corneille seems to have chosen precisely the one wrong time to remind Mazarin of his earlier close relations with the Barberini family.

6. Marie-Odile Sweetser, in her *Conceptions dramatiques de Corneille*, devotes a valuable chapter to the Examens and the *Discours* of 1660. She, too, privileges the "Discours de la tragédie" by quoting from it very extensively, especially in the last half of the chapter. She points up Corneille's independence still further by contrasting his views with those of the Abbé d'Aubignac, whose *Pratique du théâtre* had recently appeared. Corneille's modernism, so forcefully expressed in the "Discours de la tragédie," distances him from d'Aubignac at the same time that it links him to Tasso and the *Discorsi*.

7. H. B. Charlton, in *Castelvetro's Theory of Poetry*, likens Corneille and Tasso as critics with a bias: "In this respect the *Discorsi* of Tasso bear a marked resemblance to Corneille's *Examens* and his *Discours*: both Corneille and Tasso were debarred by their immediate purpose from that independence of judgment which is Castelvetro's" (p. 172). The practical experience from which Corneille and Tasso write would seem to me to compensate more than adequately for whatever weaknesses may derive from their bias.

CONCLUSION

1. By 1660, when the "Discours" appeared, Corneille may also have begun to sense an impending shift of opinion in France away from Tasso: the French epics modeled on the *Gerusalemme* had all failed, Mambrun had dared to criticize Tasso himself, etc. In time, belief in the progress of poetry and in the transference of poetic power from ancient Rome to France by way of Italy broke down altogether. In the words of Cecilia Rizza: "L'unité du monde de la culture se voit brisée et . . . dans les limites étroites de la culture littéraire la tradition humaniste prend sa fin. . . . [Désormais les partisans des Anciens] défendent la culture classique qu'ils suivent dans ses exemples les plus prestigieux, sans besoin d'aucun intermédiaire moderne . . . " ("Etat présent des études sur les rapports franco-italiens au XVIe siècle," p. 11). Corneille's emulation of Tasso, we have seen, was a reflection of the playwright's modernism. Once modernism had been called into question, it would no longer have been to his advantage to claim succession to Tasso. Such a claim would have tended to isolate him even more from the new literary scene.

BIBLIOGRAPHY

Adam, Antoine. "A travers la 'Querelle du *Cid*.'" *Revue d'Histoire de la Philosophie et d'Histoire générale de la Civilisation* [*Revue des Sciences Humaines*], 15 January 1938, pp. 29–52.

———. *Histoire de la littérature française au XVIIe siècle.* 5 vols. Paris: Del Duca, 1962.

d'Alibray, Vion, trans. *L'Aminte du Tasse.* Paris: P. Ricolet, 1632.

———, trans. *La Pompe funèbre.* Adaptation from Cremonini. Paris: P. Ricolet, 1634.

———, trans. *Le Torrismon du Tasse.* Paris: D. Houssaye, 1636.

Aristotle. *[Poetics] On the Art of Poetry.* Trans. T. S. Dorsch. In *Classical Literary Criticism.* Baltimore: Penguin Books, 1965.

d'Aumale, Le duc, ed. *Inventaire des meubles du Cardinal Mazarin.* London: Whittingham and Wilkins, 1861.

Barnwell, H. T., ed. *Pompée.* By Pierre Corneille. London: Oxford University Press, 1971.

Bartolommei, Girolamo. *Teodora* and *Polietto.* Vol. 2 of his *Tragedie.* Florence: P. Nesti, 1655.

Beall, Chandler B. *La Fortune du Tasse en France.* Eugene, Ore.: University of Oregon Press; New York: MLA, 1942.

Belliard, G., trans. *Aminte: fable boscagere du seigneur Torquato Tasso.* Rouen: Claude le Villain, 1603. (Original edition: Paris: A. l'Angelier, 1596.)

Beni, Paolo. *Comparatione di Omero, Virgiliano e Torquato et a chi di loro si debba la palma nell'heroico poema.* Padua: Pasquati, 1607.

Bénichou, Paul. *Morales du grand siècle.* Paris: Gallimard, 1948.

Boisrobert, L'abbé de. *La Vraye Didon: ou la Didon chaste.* Paris: T. Quinet, 1643.

Bray, René. *La Formation de la doctrine classique en France.* Paris: Hachette, 1927.

Brody, Jules. "Platonisme et classicisme." In *French Classicism: A Critical Miscellany*, pp. 186–207. Ed. Jules Brody. Englewood Cliffs, N.J.: Prentice-Hall, 1966.

Butler, Philip. *Classicisme et baroque dans l'oeuvre de Racine.* Paris: Nizet, 1959.

Castelvetro, Lodovico. *Poetica d'Aristotele, vulgarizzata e sposta.* Ed. Werther Romani. 2 vols. Rome-Bari: Laterza, 1979.

Chapelain, Jean. *Opuscules critiques.* Ed. Alfred C. Hunter. Société des Textes Français Modernes. Paris: Droz, 1936.

Charlton, H. B. *Castelvetro's Theory of Poetry.* Manchester, England: At the University Press, 1913.

Chéruel, A. *Histoire de France pendant la minorité de Louis XIV.* Vol. 2. Paris: Hachette, 1879.

Corneille, Pierre. *Oeuvres.* Ed. Ch. Marty-Laveaux. 12 vols. Paris: Hachette, 1862–68.

Couton, Georges. *Corneille.* Paris: Hatier, 1958.

Cremona, Isida. *L'Influence de l'Aminta sur la pastorale dramatique française.* Paris: Vrin, 1977.

Dalla Valle, Daniela. "*Le Torrismon du Tasse* par Charles Vion d'Alibray: entre tragédie et tragicomédie." *Cahiers de littérature du XVIIe siècle* (Toulouse) 6 (1984): 105–14.

Dante Alighieri. *The Convivio.* Trans. Philip H. Wicksteed. London: Dent, 1912.

————. *On World Government (De Monarchia).* Trans. Herbert W. Schneider. 2d rev. ed. New York: Liberal Arts Press, 1957.

Davis, Charles Till. *Dante and the Idea of Rome.* Oxford: Clarendon Press, 1957.

Doubrovsky, Serge. *Corneille et la dialectique du héros.* Paris: Gallimard, 1963.

Du Mas, Le sieur, trans. *Lydie: fable champestre. Imitee en partie de l'Aminthe du Torquato Tasso.* Paris: J. Millot, 1609.

Fumaroli, Marc. "Classicisme français et culture italienne: réflexions sur l'échec de *Théodore.*" In *Mélanges à la mémoire de Franco Simone,* 2:205–38. Geneva: Slatkine, 1980.

————. "Corneille, lecteur de la *Filli di Sciro.*" In *Mélanges historiques et littéraires sur le XVIIe siècle offerts à Georges Mongrédien,* pp. 313–26. Paris: Société d'Etude du XVIIe Siècle, 1974.

————. "Critique et création littéraire: J. L. Guez de Balzac et P. Corneille (1637–1645)." *Travaux de linguistique et de littérature* (Strasbourg) 13, 2 (1975): 73–89.

————. "Les Enchantements de l'éloquence; *Les Fées* de Charles Perrault ou De la littérature." In *Le Statut de la littérature: mélanges offerts à Paul Bénichou,* pp. 153–86. Ed. Marc Fumaroli. Geneva: Droz, 1982.

————. "Héroïsme cornélien et l'idéal de la magnanimité." In *Héroïsme et création littéraire sous les règnes d'Henri IV et de Louis XIII,* pp. 53–76. Ed. Noémi Hepp and Georges Livet. Paris: Klincksieck, 1974.

————. "Melpomène au miroir: la Tragédie comme héroïne." *Saggi e Ricerche di Letteratura francese* 19 (1980): 175–205.

————. "Rhétorique, dramaturgie, critique littéraire: le recours à l'allégorie dans les querelles littéraires (1578–1630)." In *Critique et création littéraire en France au XVIIe siècle,* pp. 453–72. Paris: C.N.R.S., 1974.

————. "Rhétorique et dramaturgie: le statut du personnage dans la tragédie classique." *Revue d'Histoire du Théâtre* 24 (1972): 223–50.

————. "Théâtre, humanisme et Contre-Réforme à Rome (1597–1642): l'oeuvre du P. Bernardino Stefonio et son influence." *Bulletin de l'Association G. Budé* 33 (1974): 397–412.

————. "Tragique païen et tragique chrétien dans *Rodogune.*" *Revue des Sciences Humaines,* Oct.-Dec. 1973, pp. 599–631.

Gasté, Armand, ed. *La Querelle du Cid: pièces et pamphlets.* Paris: Welter, 1898.

Genette, Gérard. *Palimpsestes: la littérature au second degré.* Paris: Editions du Seuil, 1982.

Gérard, Albert. "'Vice ou Vertu': Modes of Self-Assertion in Corneille's *La Mort de Pompée.*" *Revue des Langues Vivantes* 31 (1965): 323–52.

Greene, Thomas M. *The Descent from Heaven: A Study in Epic Continuity.* New Haven: Yale University Press, 1963.

Guarini, Giovanni Battista. *Il Pastor fido.* Ed. G. Brognoligo. Bari: Laterza, 1914.

Guitton, Jean. "Les Aspects religieux de *Polyeucte.*" In *Polyeucte martyr* (monograph prepared by Sylvie Chevalley for the 648th representation of the play), pp. 24–30. Paris: Comédie Française, 1960.

Herland, Louis. *Corneille par lui-même.* Paris: Editions du Seuil, 1966.

————. "Les Eléments précornéliens dans *La Mort de Pompée* de Corneille." *Revue d'Histoire Littéraire de la France* 50 (1950): 1–15.

La Mothe le Vayer, François de. *De la vertu des payens.* In *Oeuvres.* Vol. 2. Geneva: Slatkine Reprints, 1970.

Lancaster, Henry Carrington. *A History of French Dramatic Literature in the Seventeenth Century.* 8 vols. Baltimore: The Johns Hopkins University Press, 1929–40.

Lewis, C. S. "Historicism." In *God, History, and Historians: An Anthology of Modern Christian Views of History,* pp. 225–38. Ed. C. I. McIntire. New York: Oxford University Press, 1977.

Loukovitch, Kosta. *L'Evolution de la tragédie religieuse classique en France.* Paris: Droz, 1933.

Lucan. *Pharsalia: Dramatic Episodes of the Civil War.* Trans. Robert Graves. Baltimore: Penguin Books, 1957.

Macrobius. *The Saturnalia.* Trans. Percival V. Davies. New York: Columbia University Press, 1969.

Maskell, David. *The Historical Epic in France: 1500–1700.* London: Oxford University Press, 1973.

Maurens, Jacques. *La Tragédie sans tragique: le Néo-stoïcisme dans l'oeuvre de Pierre Corneille.* Paris: Colin, 1966.

May, Georges. *Tragédie cornélienne, tragédie racinienne: étude sur les sources de l'intérêt dramatique.* Illinois Studies in Language and Literature, Vol. 32, No. 4. Urbana: University of Illinois Press, 1948.

Mazarin, homme d'état et collectionneur, 1602–1661. Exposition organisée pour le troisième centenaire de sa mort. Paris: Bibliothèque Nationale, 1961.

Mongrédien, Georges. *Recueil des textes et des documents du XVIIᵉ siècle relatifs à Corneille.* Paris: C.N.R.S., 1972.

Nelson, Robert J. *Corneille: His Heroes and Their Worlds.* Philadelphia: University of Pennsylvania Press, 1963.

Nicole, Pierre. *Traité de la comédie.* Ed. Georges Couton. Paris: Les Belles Lettres, 1961.

Pavel, Thomas G. *La Syntaxe narrative des tragédies de Corneille.* Paris: Klincksieck, 1976.

Pellisson-Fontanier, Paul, and Pierre Joseph Thorellier d'Olivet. *Histoire de l'Académie française.* 2 vols. Ed. Ch.-L. Livet. Paris: Didier, 1858.

Perrault, Charles. *Les Hommes illustres qui ont paru en France pendant ce siècle.* Vol. 1. Paris: Dezallier, 1697; rpt. Geneva: Slatkine Reprints, 1970.

Petrarch, F. *The Triumphs.* Trans. Ernest Hatch Wilkins. Chicago: University of Chicago Press, 1962.

Pintard, René. "Un témoignage sur *Le Cid,* en 1637." In *Mélanges d'histoire littéraire de la Renaissance offerts à Henri Chamard,* pp. 292–301. Paris: Nizet, 1951.

Poirier, Germain. *Corneille et la vertu de prudence.* Geneva: Droz, 1984.

Quinet, T. (?), trans. *L'Amynte.* Paris: T. Quinet, 1638.

Rayssiguier, Le sieur de, trans. *L'Aminte du Tasse.* Paris: Courbé, 1632.

Riddle, Lawrence M. *The Genesis and Sources of Pierre Corneille's Tragedies from Médée to Pertharite.* Baltimore: The Johns Hopkins University Press, 1926.

Rizza, Cecilia. "Etat présent des études sur les rapports franco-italiens au XVIIᵉ siècle." In *L'Italianisme en France au XVIIᵉ siècle.* Ed. Giorgio Mirandola. Supplement to *Studi Francese* 35 (May-August 1968): 11–19.

Sainte-Beuve, C.-A. *Causeries du lundi.* Vol. 9. Paris: Garnier, [1854].

Scudéry, Georges de. *Didon.* Paris: Courbé, 1637.

Searles, Colbert. "Italian Influences as seen in the Sentiments of the French Academy on the *Cid.*" *Romanic Review* 3 (1912): 362–90.

Sellstrom, A. Donald. "Comedy in *Théodore* and Beyond." In *Corneille comique: Nine Studies of Pierre Corneille's Comedy.* Ed. Milorad R. Margitic. Tübingen: Biblio 17 (Supplement to *Papers on French Seventeenth Century Literature*), 1982, pp. 169–83.

———. "Corneille, émule du Tasse." In *Pierre Corneille: Actes du Colloque,* pp. 137–44. Paris: Presses Universitaires de France, 1986.

———. "*L'Illusion comique* of Corneille: The Tragic Scenes of Act V." *Modern Language Notes* 73 (1958): 421–27.

———. "*La Mort de Pompée*: Roman History and Tasso's Theory of Christian Epic." *PMLA* 97 (1982): 830–43.

———. "La *Théodore* de Corneille ou le statut social de l'écrivain." In *Le Mécénat en France avant Colbert (1598–1661),* pp. 209–18. Paris: C.N.R.S., 1985.

Simpson, Joyce G. *Le Tasse et la littérature et l'art baroques en France.* Paris: Nizet, 1962.

Stegmann, André. "L'Ambiguïté du concept héroïque dans la littérature morale en France sous Louis XIII." In *Héroïsme et création littéraire sous les règnes d'Henri IV et de Louis XIII,* pp. 29–51. Ed. Noémi Hepp and Georges Livet. Paris: Klincksieck, 1974.

———. *L'Héroïsme cornélien: genèse et signification.* 2 vols. Paris: Colin, 1968.

Sweetser, Marie-Odile. *Les Conceptions dramatiques de Corneille.* Geneva: Droz, 1962.

———. "La Conversion du prince: réflexions sur la tragédie providentielle." *Papers on French Seventeenth Century Literature* 19 (1983): 497–510.

———. "Corneille et la tragédie providentielle: la conversion." *Cahiers de l'Association internationale des études françaises* 37 (1985): 163–76.

———. *La Dramaturgie de Corneille.* Geneva: Droz, 1977.

———. "La Femme abandonnée: esquisse d'une typologie." *Papers on French Seventeenth Century Literature* 10 (1978–79): 143–78.

———. "Images de la femme abandonnée: traditions, contaminations, créations." In *Onze nouvelles études sur l'image de la femme dans la littérature française du dix-septième siècle,* pp. 1–11. Ed. Wolfgang Leiner. Tübingen: Gunter Narr; Paris: Jean-Michel Place, 1984.

———. "Place de l'amour dans la hiérarchie des valeurs cornéliennes." *Travaux de linguistique et de littérature* (Strasbourg) 20, 2 (1982): 63–77.

———. "Tragic Situation and Providential Intervention: The Case for a New Concept of Tragedy in 17th-Century French Theatre." *Seventeenth-Century French Studies* 7 (1985): 65–73.

Tasso, Torquato. *The Aminta.* Trans. Louis E. Lord. Published together with *The Orpheus* of Angelo Politian. Oxford: Oxford University Press; London: Humphrey Milford, 1931.

———. *Apologia in difesa della Gerusalemme liberata.* In *Torquato Tasso: Scritti sull'arte poetica,* pp. 65–139. Ed. Ettore Mazzoli. Turin: Einaudi, 1977.

———. "De la vertu des dames illustres." In *Les Morales du Tasse.* Trans. Jean Baudoin. Paris: du Bray et Courbé, 1632.

———. *Discorsi dell'arte poetica e del poema eroico.* Ed. Luigi Poma. Bari: Laterza, 1964.

————. *Discourses on the Heroic Poem*. Trans. Mariella Cavalchini and Irene Samuel. Oxford: Clarendon Press, 1973.

————. "Du poëme heroïque." In *Recueil d'emblemes divers*, pp. 577–619. Trans. Jean Baudoin. Paris: Villery, 1639.

————. *Il Goffredo, overo la Gierusalemme liberata del Tasso, col Commento del Beni*. Padua: Bolgetta, 1616.

————. *Opere*. Ed. Bartolo Tommaso Sozzi. 2 vols. Turin: Unione Tipographico-Editrice Torinese, 1974.

Vedel, Valdemar. *Deux classiques français vus par un critique étranger*. Paris: Champion, 1935.

Vergil. *The Aeneid of Virgil*. Trans. Rolfe Humphries. New York: Scribner's, 1951.

————. *Publi Vergili Maronis Aeneidos Liber Quartus*. Ed. Arthur S. Pease. Darmstadt: Wissenschaftliche Buchgesellschaft, 1967. (Originally published Boston: Harvard University Press, 1935.)

Voltaire. "Commentaires sur Corneille." In *Oeuvres complètes*. Vol 21. Ed. Beuchot-Moland. Paris: Garnier, 1880.

Weinberg, Bernard. *A History of Literary Criticism in the Italian Renaissance*. 2 vols. Chicago: University of Chicago Press, 1961.

Williamson, Edouard. *Les Meubles d'art du Mobilier national*. 2 vols. Paris: Baudry, 1883.

INDEX

WESTFIELD UNIV. LONDON COLLEGE

WITHDRAWN
FROM STOCK
QMUL LIBRARY